From *the* TRENCHES

N. S. Jordan

Copyright © 2018 N. S. Jordan
All rights reserved
First Edition

PAGE PUBLISHING, INC.
New York, NY

First originally published by Page Publishing, Inc. 2018

This publication is based on some historical characters and events. Some names have been altered for this publication. Some readers may find some language offensive and or some events disturbing.

ISBN 978-1-64298-154-4 (Paperback)
ISBN 978-1-64298-155-1 (Digital)

Printed in the United States of America

From murder, suicide, fires, floods, and ghosts.
To crazy animals and quirky people.
I guess you could say that I've seen it all, but there's always new adventure waiting inside . . .

The memoirs of N. S. Jordan and her personal experiences and professional forty-year escapade as real estate sales agent and rental property manager.

To my late mother-in-law, Anna Mae Jordan, for your perseverance in my becoming a Realtor.

Preface

The Irony of It All

At a very young age, I realized that people sometimes would react in unexpected ways to certain situations.

I am the youngest of three siblings My late brother, Terry, may God rest his soul, was twelve years older than I, and my little big sister, Karen, is eight years older. I say "little" big sister because I am a head taller than she.

It was then that I learned about irony—the inappropriate reaction between the actual and expected result of events.

It was 1962. Just five years old, I was merrily riding my stick horse all along the big gravel driveways of the Silver Moon Motel that my parents owned and operated, when my legs became tangled and I fell to the ground. I didn't cry; in fact, I wasn't even hurt. I was about to get up when I noticed my dad running toward me. Kenny, my dad, was a nice-looking man with dark wavy hair and was in his midforties. He was always dressed in his dark blue work uniform and always had a cigarette in his mouth, which is how he eventually met his demise. He ran toward me to pick me up out of the gravel and brush me off, or so one would think that's what he was going to do. Instead, without saying a word, he grabbed my beloved stick horse off the ground, broke it over his knee, threw it to the ground, turned, and walked away. It only took me fifty years to finally realize that he did it to protect me from getting hurt.

As a teenager, I became a young bride and mother. My mother-in-law, a Realtor herself, was persistent in that I go to school, get my real estate license, and become a Realtor. And from that moment on, I realized that shit happens, that popular observation that bad things happen for no reason. But it always just seemed like more shit happened to me! In my twenties, I had my very first paranormal experiences selling real estate. In my thirties, I began to manage rental properties and really began to discover the irony of it all. In my forties, I became a grandmother. And by the time I reached my fifties, so many wild and crazy escapades had happened to me in my personal life and forty-plus-year career in real estate that every now and then, when reminded of one my escapades, I would tell a story and someone would say, "You should write a book." Then one fall day, something happened that changed everything and I decided I had to tell my stories.

Funny thing, though. Even one's reaction to those four words "I'm writing a book" is ironic. There are two reactions: There's the positive one when people say encouraging words like "Great," "Awesome," "I think you should!" Then there's the reaction where they don't say a word and just look at me like I have two heads.

Oh, the irony of it all

Sticks and Stones

The age of email, voicemail, and texting—allowing a person to say what they wouldn't dare say to your face through the use of so many different portals! The following is a little medley of the names that were called and things people have said to me since the dawn of technology.

I've been called . . .

Anal, incompetent, stereotyping, discriminating, high-end ass, lying, thieving scumbag, backstabbing, pathetic princess, dishonest, sad slumlord, rude, unethical, combative, jerk, and you better watch your back. Last but not least—You will pay for your kindness in full. Open the door, karma is knocking.

Incompetent and backstabbing? A young gal who was living in a condo that I managed failed to have the water and sewer service put into her name. A year or so went by when it was brought to my attention. When I in turn brought the delinquent water and sewer bill to her attention, which had grown to be over $1,000, she told me in a voice mail that I was backstabbing and incompetent. Me? I was the incompetent one? And who was the backstabber? I had even gotten all her late fees removed!

Lying, thieving, scumbag, dishonest, sad slumlord. I received this title via email because a security deposit wasn't returned to the tenant due to the family's cocker spaniel having urinated on the entire main level carpet of a two-story home that required a complete carpet replacement. Eventually, lying, thieving, scumbag became my loving nicknames among some of my coworkers. Whenever I would complain of a tenant or landlord, Wendy would never miss the opportunity to say, "Well, you know that you are a lying, thieving scumbag, LOL."

High-end ass; rude, pathetic princess! All because I refused to allow a couple with bad credit and two large dogs look at a home that was being advertised for lease. The property had nearly new carpet in it and just happened to be the home where my husband and I had raised our family and lived for twenty-nine years. Why would I settle for two large dogs and bad credit?

Jerk, something that I thought that you'd call a guy. In a text message, a guy told me that I was a jerk because we wouldn't reimburse him $600 for a stone landscaping wall that he installed without permission on the side of the property he was renting. I was the jerk?

Anal, because a tenant didn't receive her security and pet deposit refund. If I'm anal because I didn't think she should let her dogs pee on the interior and exterior doors so much that the metal doors were rusted off at the bottom and wooden doors swollen. Anal, because I found a dead snake next to her cat's scratching post. Anal, because there was an outline of a dead dog on the garage floor and the same under the basement stairs with cat fur still stuck to the concrete floor. Well, yeah, then yes, I guess I am pretty anal.

After returning from an eviction, I came back to my office to hear a voicemail from someone claiming to be a friend of the family that I had just evicted. The voice mail simply said, **"You better watch your back."** And I did too! Every evening for weeks, I would have someone watch me walk out to my car.

After learning there would be no refund of a security and pet deposit, the voice on the message said, **"You will pay for your kindness in full. Open the door, karma is knocking."** An older woman and teenage daughter had been asked to move because the owner of the property needed to sell. The tenant had removed the hallway carpet because her pets had ruined it and then left the house in shambles. The house was such a mess, the landlord refused to make repairs or turn on the heat, so the pipes froze and the bank foreclosed. Guess we opened the door and karma did come knocking.

Discriminating and unethical? Please be the judge. After showing a couple one house, they applied to rent the property, but they were declined by the landlord due to a poor credit history, and the landlord accepted another applicant with much better credit. A short time later, a discrimination complaint was filed alleging that I had shown the couple six properties in some other area that I have never even worked in, and they said that I had turned their application down for every single property that I had shown them. Hello! I showed them one house that wasn't far from my office, just one house. Unethical? What those people put me through was immoral!

Combative, after insisting to the heirs of a tenant who had passed away, their attorney and the auctioneer…a public estate auction could not be held in or at the rental home…the attorney accused me of being combative. No way I would want a hundred strangers in my house! Would you?

Caller: I'm disabled, and I need an apartment.
Me: The only apartments I have right now are townhomes.
Caller: Now you're *stereotyping*.
Me: I was just letting you know the type of apartments that we have available, at this time.
Caller: You are *rude*.
Click

That old children's rhyme? Sticks and stones may break my bones, but words will never hurt me? Well, words may not hurt physically, but they certainly do sting just a little.

Things That Go Bump
in
The Night

The Attic Room

I've had many intriguing experiences during my forty-year real estate career. This is the first of many true stories about some pretty strange happenings surrounding a few of the old houses in my home town of Saint Charles.

With its historic Main Street, ten blocks long and over two hundred years old, it is situated on the banks of the Missouri River. First settled in the late 1700s by a French-Canadian fur trader who named the settlement Les Petite Cotes. "The Little Hills."

With its quaint old shops along the redbrick streets, Main Street St. Charles has always drawn quite a crowd on Saturday and Sunday afternoons. One can take a bicycle ride, a leisurely stroll on the Katy Trail or an afternoon carriage ride along the river. Listen to the music being played in the bandstand at Frontier park or relax on an outdoor patio at one of the local wineries. Take in the "Festival of the Little Hills" while enjoying a yummy funnel cake and maybe even find a treasure, handmade by the local craftsmen. Some 300,000 visitors attend the three-day event every year.

Why you can even take an evening walking tour of some historic places in the Main Street district. The advertisement for the tour claimed that you might encounter a mysterious manifestation, visit places to have reported ghostly activity, unexplained noises and even ghostly smells. "Will you see a glimpse of a roaming spirit who was a victim of a tragic death or be grabbed from behind by one of the old souls from the lost graveyard?" The grave markers were moved in 1853, but the bodies were left behind . . .

That's one sightseeing tour I won't be caught dead on . . . why pay to get the crap scared out of me, when I can get it for free!

Which brings to mind one particular old house that I will never forget. It wasn't located in the Main Street District but it certainly had its own share of intriguing and unexplained manifestations.

Built in the Roaring Twenties, the house was a one-and-a-half-story-style home. A style that was commonly found in the Old Town district of our city, bordered by both the Missouri and Mississippi Rivers. The Wide Missouri and Muddy Mississippi, if you will.

The old house was painted white with light blue trim and almost always was in need of some TLC.

It had wooden steps leading up to brick columns with white spindled handrails that surrounded the expansive covered porch, which spanned the entire front of the house.

John was an absentee landlord that lived out of state. He had inherited two homes that had been in his family for years, and the pair happened to be right next door to one another.

John had grown up in the white house with blue trim, and his aunt and uncle had lived next door.

The house next door was a one-and-a-half-story style as well. It looked a lot like John's parents' home, but it was much larger and painted all white.

Both were occupied with tenants. However, living so far away, John enlisted my company's services to manage the two properties.

Two years passed before a man by the name of Mack, who had been renting the house where John grew up, decided to move out. I had never even met this man; he was very elusive. In fact, I had never even spoken to him.

I would send late notice after late notice, pleading with him to at least call to let me know when I could expect the rent. Then when I'd least expect it, he would deposit the rent through the slot in the front door of my office sometime during the night.

One day, the rent payments stopped coming in. I spent several hours just trying to figure out if Mack was still living there or not.

The curtains were drawn tight and the house was always dark at night. No one had seen him come or go for a while now. And he certainly had not told a soul that he was leaving.

After investigating the situation for several days, I decided to go ahead and have my locksmith meet me at the house.

My locksmith, Mr. Farland, was getting up in years, but he still managed to run his part-time locksmith service.

Mr. Farland quickly picked the lock on the front door and swung it open. Immediately I noticed the living room was full of furniture, and it had that "old house" smell. As I walked down the hallway to the kitchen, I could see that the sink was filled with dirty dishes. Upstairs the bedroom closets were empty. There were no clothes in the chest of drawers, and the bed looked like someone had just rolled out of it. No, literally—the first time I saw the bed, it almost looked like an impression was in it, but the next time I saw it, the impression was gone. But this was my very first encounter with the family-owned home, and so I didn't think much of it at the time.

It seemed as though Mack had taken what he wanted and had left in a hurry!

He had moved out all right, but he didn't tell anyone that he was leaving and he had left most of his personal belongings behind. It was almost like he had just picked up and moved out in the middle of the night. As if someone or something had driven him away.

Of course, there was a protocol that had to be followed before I could legally dispose of Mack's personal belongings. Certified letters had to be sent and an abandoned property notice had to be posted on the door.

It was several weeks before maintenance could begin the task of cleaning up. The house had been left in a mess, but we quickly got it cleaned out, cleaned up, and painted, and we're back in business again, or so I thought.

It wasn't until Mack had moved out that I realized there was more to this family-owned home than met the eye!

I had made an appointment one morning to show the house to a prospective tenant. We had arranged to meet in front of the house at 2:00 p.m. It was beginning to mist-rain, so I decided just to wait in the car until my appointment showed up. Well, after waiting twenty minutes, it became apparent to me that most likely I had been stood up! I had a feeling that I should just check on things since I was already there. It was raining by now, so I grabbed my umbrella and walked up the steps and onto the big front porch. I put the key in the lock and opened the door. As I stepped inside the door, I couldn't help but notice a large dark circle in the middle of the living room floor. The circle was about two feet in diameter and it was black. The old wooden floor had been charred, as if someone had built a fire on it!

Scared to death, I slowly eased back out the front door and on to the porch. I quietly closed the door and tiptoed down the stairs. Then I ran as fast as I could, in my high heels with umbrella in hand, down the sidewalk to my car!

I drove to the nearest pay phone to call the police.

"Emergency," the police dispatcher said.

"Hi, this is Ms. Jordan, I think a house that I manage has been vandalized. Can you please send an officer?"

When I drove up in front of the house, I could see there was already a police officer waiting on the front porch in his long raincoat, and thin clear plastic covered his hat. As I was climbing the front steps, the officer asked, "Do you have a key?"

I looked up at him and replied, "Yes, sir, I do." I waved it around up in the air to show him.

"Does anyone else have a key?" he asked.

Handing him the key so that he could unlock the door, I shook my head no. "I had all the locks changed after the last tenant moved out."

Just like in the movies, he threw open the door and shouted, *"Police! Is anyone inside!"* There wasn't a sound. No one was there.

As we cautiously entered the house, we noticed immediately that there was more damage than just the charred living room floor.

There was a huge hole that had been bashed in the hallway leading to the kitchen. It was the size of a body, like someone had been shoved into the wall. Broken pieces of plaster littered the wood floor. The officer climbed the staircase leading to the second floor with me close behind, very close behind! The smell of charred wood filled the staircase.

We carefully peered into the first bedroom on the left, which faced the front of the house. It too had a large blackened and charred circle in the middle of its wood floor. Unlike the living room, the bedroom floor was burned beyond repair.

As we crept along, passing the small alcove to the closed attic room door, we could see inside of the bedroom at the end of the hall. The floor and walls seemed to be unharmed, but there was some sort of a white substance oozing down the bedroom door.

Now the only thing left to check out was the attic room. The door to the attic room was in a small alcove just off the main hallway. The officer rapidly swung open the door. "Police!" But the room was empty. The only thing amiss was a baseball-size hole in one of the windowpanes. As we were leaving the room, we noticed something written on one of the walls.

"God cannot destroy what lives hear." *Here* was misspelled and it looked like the writing had been there for years. You know how ink looks on paper when it gets wet? How it just kind of bleeds?

Coming back down the stairs, I caught a glimpse of something else scrawled on the wall right next to the front door.

I couldn't believe my own eyes. Scratched on the wall with what appeared to have been some of the charred wood, most likely from the burned bedroom floor upstairs, was "You will never sell this house. I will always be here."

Funny, it's been twenty years since my experience, and I still get goose bumps, chills, and tears in my eyes every time I tell the story.

Creepy, to say the least!

With me sticking to the police officer like glue, we checked every window and every door, but they were all locked. None of them were broken and there was no sign of forced entry. I asked the officer if he would go to a few of the neighboring homes to ask if anyone had seen or heard anything. He began giving me excuses of why it wouldn't do any good. I guess he saw the confused look on my face and finally agreed.

He walked down the sidewalk and up the front steps of the home that was located to the left of the rental house. As I sat in my car anxiously waiting, he knocked on the front door several times and shouted "Police!" but no one came to the door.

That was it! He didn't go to any of the other houses. He just got back in his patrol car and drove away.

"You're kidding me!" I thought. "He's just going to leave me here?"

I never heard another word about it and the mystery was never solved. That day only one patrol car responded to my call, and it was clear to me that the officer didn't want to go to even one house to question the neighbors.

Just a couple of months before, I had discovered that a vacant house had been vandalized and at least five patrol cars responded!

Located in an upscale neighborhood, some kids had broken in to the vacant house through a basement window. It was a beautiful ranch-style home, situated on a three-acre lot overlooking a small subdivision lake. All the lovely kitchen cabinetry had been spray-painted with black and orange spray paint as well as the massive floor-to-ceiling white stone fireplace. Charred wood from the fireplace had been used to make a mess of the light-colored great room carpeting. Black arrows spray-painted on the light tan carpeting led the way down the hall to the bedrooms where painted on the walls was "The Bloods and Crips."

During that time, the Bloods and the Crips" happened to be gangs that were prominent in California, thousands of miles away from the mid-Missouri town where this home was located.

No, it was clear that this was just a simple case of neighborhood kids that had way too much time on their hands.

Several police cars responded to the emergency call that day. One officer assessed the damage and took my statement. The others scoured the neighborhood going door to door, looking for any information that might help them find the little darlings that vandalized this quarter-million-dollar home. My point being, it just goes to show that money talks. You know the old cliché.

Anyway, not long after repairing the plaster walls and refinishing the wood floors at the old house, a young couple fell in love with it. After all, it was a charming old home with a lot of character. A little too much character. In fact, maybe "character" was not exactly the best word to describe that house at all as you will soon learn.

After only two weeks, I found a note in the middle of my desk with the keys to the house lying on top when I returned from lunch one day.

The note simply read, "Sorry, but we had to move." The young couple left no other explanation and no way for me to reach them.

However, a few months later, the couple contacted me to ask for the return of their security deposit. They still refused to give any explanation as to why they skipped out after only two weeks.

I couldn't refund their deposit. They had failed to fulfill their lease agreement. They hadn't even fulfilled the first month! Besides, there had been expenses, like removing the fence they had built for their dog, which had been installed over the property line. The usual trash from moving had been left behind and the house wasn't exactly left in "hotel clean" condition (which by now is what I felt like I was running—a hotel!).

With nothing else left to do, I immediately put the For Rent sign back in the yard and began advertising for a new tenant.

It was now early fall and it wasn't long before Renee saw my advertisement and applied to rent the old house.

She was thirty-something and frail-looking and had long, very thin dishwater-blond hair. Renee had been commuting some 160 miles to work every day.

She thought the house was charming and just couldn't wait to move in. Only four months had gone by, and Renee came by my office to return the keys to the house one Friday afternoon.

"I had to move out. I can't say why." The owner can keep my deposit. "I just can't stay there," Renee said sorrily.

She seemed upset and left my office in a rush. By now, I was beginning to wonder. Maybe the house really did just have a little too much character, and it really wasn't as charming as everyone thought after all. If you know what I mean.

I didn't have a clue as to what to do, but the next family to move into the house certainly did.

The very next morning, after Renee turned in the keys, I received a call from a woman who was looking for a place to rent for just a short time.

The woman said just the night before a fire had damaged their home that was located near the rental house.

The location was just perfect. The kids wouldn't have to change schools, and their fire-damaged home was located nearby. They would be close to home, and it would be easy to check on the progress the workmen were making.

And so, the family moved right in to the house. Almost immediately, strange things began to go bump in the night. You can probably imagine what happened next, can't you? By now, everyone in my office knew about the strange chain of events surrounding that house.

As I came in the front door to the office early one morning, Peggy, our office secretary, with a sympathetic look on her face, said, "You have customers waiting for you in your office already."

I peered around the corner and could see the woman sitting in a chair, all bundled up in her coat.

As I entered my office, Douglas, the young agent I shared my office with (little did I know that he would eventually be the owner of the company), said with a humorous look on his face, "These people are here to see you about their lease."

The woman had brought the whole family with her to see me—her husband and three children—and they all looked like they had seen a ghost!

"Good morning. What can I do for you guys?"

They didn't waste any time getting right to the point.

"Is there any way we can get out of our lease?" the woman asked.

"Can I ask why?"

For a moment, the man and woman stared at one another, and then the man finally broke the silence.

"I work a lot of nights and every morning when I get home, I find my family asleep in the living room."

"We can't sleep upstairs," the woman said.

I had a pretty good idea but asked anyway, "Why not?"

She became upset and began to explain. "Every night. It happens every night. About 1:00 a.m., we hear what sounds like a man and a woman screaming at each other! It sounds like it's coming from inside the attic room. And they're fighting or something, but you can't really tell what they are saying."

Listening to her story, I wondered about the window in the attic having been broken and the writing on the wall with the misspelled words.

I shuddered to think, "Was this why Mack moved so suddenly and why no one ever stayed more than a few months or weeks even?" It all seemed to fall into place.

Suddenly, it came over me—goose bumps, chills, and tears in my eyes. Trying not to let them see that I was a bit unnerved by their story, I calmly said, "Let me call the owner. I'll make him aware of your concerns about the house, and I'll be back in touch with you in a few days."

The very moment the couple and their family left my office, I was on the phone calling John.

I really had no idea what I was going to say to him. So I just told him everything. About the screams that were heard coming from the attic room. The voices of a man and of a woman. The fighting.

He chuckled and said, "That sounds like Mom and Dad."

Again, I was at a loss for words. I didn't expect to hear him say that!

Just then, a question came to mind. I wasn't sure if I should ask it, but what the heck, I asked anyway.

"Did your parents pass away in the house?"

"Yes, as a matter of fact they did."

"Oh . . . well! Okay then."

I wasn't expecting John to be quite so blunt with his answer. Don't ask me why, but I wasn't quite expecting his answer to be yes either!

"What should I tell your tenants about breaking the lease?"

He said what many of my landlords say whenever they don't want to make a decision.

"Whatever you want to do, I'll leave it up to you."

"That's just great. Now what am I going to do?" I thought.

I'd say that I got out of the situation that I had found myself in pretty easily. Because before I even had a chance to call the tenants back, they called me and let me off the hook.

"We have spoken to a priest," the woman said. "We are going to have the house blessed."

"OK?" I thought. "Like an exorcism!"

After the blessing, a rosary was affixed to the attic room door, and no one ever mentioned any more occurrences at the house.

In fact, after the family had moved back in to their home, a stern old woman by the name of Opal lived in the house for nearly ten years after.

She lived there until John decided to sell both of his rental properties.

This time *I* was actually going to get to ask someone to move out of the house for a change.

I was giving someone notice to move.

Maybe the blessing of the house worked, or maybe the beings in the attic room were no match for Opal.

I think most likely, the latter of the two. As some fourteen years after the blessing of the house took place, I learned through a newspaper article that the blessing really hadn't worked at all.

In early October, I was contacted by a local newspaper reporter. He was known for his weekly column.

With Halloween fast approaching, the reporter was very persistent. He had called several times and had left messages saying that he wanted to interview me about the two family-owned homes.

By this time, Douglas was no longer one of my coagents. He was now my manager and co-owner of the company.

We had already sold the house that John had grown up in. However, Douglas had shown the reporter and his wife, Johns aunts house that had been for sale and was just as creepy as you will later learn.

I hesitated to do the interview, just as I had when a group who claimed to research the paranormal had contacted me several years ago.

One day I got a call from an out of state firm. Their specialty was researching the paranormal. They actually wanted to set up their equipment inside the house next door to record any paranormal activity.

"No way," I said. "I'll never be able to rent the house again or sell it for that matter," I thought.

The man understood my position and didn't pursue it much further.

I tried to ignore the reporter's phone call, but he was persistent and I finally gave in.

I explained to him that I didn't want my name or the company where I worked to appear in the paper. Plain and simple, I didn't want people to think I was nuts! With the ground rules laid, I agreed to do the interview.

Well, it was Halloween and the paper hit the streets. Sure enough, the article was in it.

I was a little disappointed though. There was very little mention about me in the article after all!

Fourteen years later, I had led the reporter to the family that had lived in the house that had it blessed, and the story was all about them!

The family shared stories with the reporter that even I had never heard before, and so the story goes like this . . .

The Examination of a Ghost Story

What really happened?
    I'm going to do what reporters often do. I'm going to check out a story. In this case, a ghost story.

This story came to me on a personal level. It wasn't pitched, for example, by a restaurateur who wants the whole world to know his establishment is haunted.

As you will find out, my reporting led me to a family that rented the house fourteen years ago in St. Charles where they say, strange things happened.

In 2003, my wife and I were house hunting in St. Charles. One of the houses we looked at was near the high school.

My real estate agent, Douglas, who is also a friend and a reliable guy, when things go bump in the night, is more likely to think of squirrels than ghosts.

He told me his company for several years had managed the house he was showing me, as well as one next door, and that the owner of both of these houses lived out of state.

The strange thing, my real estate agent said, was various people, from different tenants to different maintenance workers, independently had reported creepy things next door.

All these ghostly tales were reported to the same person. She handles the rental property for the real estate company.

She didn't want her name in the paper. She was afraid people would think she's nuts. She also didn't give the address of the house, but actually I learned of the two houses.

Finally, you probably also should know this about her. She says she has had other paranormal experiences unrelated to the houses as well.

I won't quote her, but where's the impact of an anonymous source telling secondhand ghost stories?

But an important thing I did learn from her is the ghost stories involved not only the house next to the one my real estate agent showed me but also the very house I looked at!

She helped me get in touch with Dale, now seventy-four years old. He remembers working in the basement of one of the houses when it was vacant years ago.

"I was working on the furnace in the basement," he said. "I heard a woman's voice singing. My guess was that one of the real estate agents were upstairs."

The voice was beautiful, he recalled. But every time he went upstairs, the singing stopped. No one was there.

That's the story. I asked Dale if it was a ghost.

"I don't know. I do know that I had a weird feeling when I heard it for a second time," he said.

He also says he has had other paranormal experiences.

Through public records, I learned a little bit about the family.

A newspaper story states that one of the girls made the All-District Choir while a student at the high school.

She told me that she sang a lot while living in the house next to the one where Dale heard that mysterious female voice.

Did he hear the girl and not a ghost? I think it's possible. But what's more difficult to explain, unless you question the family's credibility, is what they said occurred in the other house. The family lived there for four to six months with their three children.

They agreed to be interviewed.

The husband initially had no recollection of anything unusual at the house. But he did recall the blessing of the house by a priest.

"I was a truck driver and I wasn't home a lot," he said.

The family moved to the rental home after a fire damaged their house and caused $30,000 in damage to their home.

"The very first night, I was in the basement putting a load of laundry in the washer. I felt a hand on my shoulder," said the missus. "There was no one there," she said.

"I reached for the washing machine dial and something grabbed my arm—hard," she said.

At a later date, while trying to comfort her daughter, she said she was grabbed so hard, she was bruised. She reported her concerns to her husband. "He just said I was stressed out."

She and her daughters said, yes, they were stressed out. They had lost all their possessions in the fire, but the stress level skyrocketed once they moved into the rental house.

I told the missus that if an invisible force had grabbed my arm and left bruises, then I would leave, pronto!

"There was no place to go," she explained. The flood of '93 had made rental housing scarce.

One of the daughters said she was alone in her upstairs bedroom one night when she felt the air pressure change.

"It's like the air gets condensed," she said. "I felt like something touched my hair. I could not move because I was so afraid. I have never been so afraid before or since then."

Another daughter said she felt a hand push her down the stairs. She also recounted the time she was in her bedroom when something seemed to kick the door open. A footprint was left on the door, she said. Yet no one was there.

Eventually both girls abandoned their upstairs bedrooms. One slept on a love seat downstairs and the other stayed with friends. Their brother slept on a sofa sleeper downstairs.

One of the girls also recalled the door to the attic would open by itself. They put a latch on it.

The attic was an unfinished area on the same level as the two bedrooms.

In the attic, she discovered writing in red letters: "God cannot destroy what lives here."

I asked if she knew it was there because she wrote it.

"No," she said.

It was one of the girls who called the priest—not because the family is Catholic but because she knew from watching movies that he might be able to help.

She did not initially tell the priest the family thought the house was haunted.

"I figured he wouldn't believe me and he wouldn't come."

Once the priest arrived, she told him of the strange happenings and asked him to bless the basement and the attic.

But the disturbing events just continued after the blessing.

"I couldn't take it anymore," she said. Two weeks before the lease was up, they moved back into their house. Even though the repair work wasn't finished, they lived in the basement.

The missus rarely talks about her terrifying experiences in the rental house. "People just kind of look at you, kind of like the way you're looking at me now," she said.

John, seventy-eight, who lives out of state, owned both of the houses. He grew up in one, and his aunt and uncle lived in the other.

He has no firsthand knowledge of anything unusual occurring in either house. The only ghost stories he has ever heard were the ones relayed to him by the person who managed the properties for him.

I knocked on the door of one of the houses and the current renter said he knows of nothing unusual. Neither does the owner or previous owner.

"The house is too young to be haunted," said the owner, "It's only sixty-five years old. So give me a break."

Another family now lived in the home once rented. They bought it four years ago. I asked him so that his young daughter wouldn't overhear. He said there's been nothing unusual. "But after talking to you, I'm going to be up tonight freaking out," he said.

Then the owner said there was one oddity. Someone had attached a lock to the outside of the door to the attic, as if to lock something inside.

He let me look at the attic. There's the lock on the door, but I told him that I couldn't find what I was looking for—the writing on the wall.

It's in red: "God can't destroy what lives hear!"

I immediately notice the misspelling of "here." But who says ghosts are good spellers?

The new owner had noticed the writing before but didn't think much of it. "But I'm not going to lie to you," he said. "It seems to be darker than when I first saw it."

Well, if you happened to read the article online, you could also voice your opinion in the comments section. One of the daughters did just that.

She wrote, "The story was good. But if you ever want to do a follow-up, let me know. There is a lot more to the story. I wonder if the children that live in the house now have ever seen or heard anything or they just didn't want to share?"

When interviewed, John may have pretended to know nothing, but I think that he must have remembered something.

He at least knew that I went above and beyond (no pun intended) to take care of the properties that had been in his family for years.

Every year just before Christmas, he would order up the biggest Red Poinsettia from the most expensive florist in town, and the flowers just got bigger and more beautiful every year.

The Flirtatious One

By now, you should at least be somewhat familiar with "the house next door." Remember? John's aunt and uncle lived in the house next to the one where he had grown up.

Nettie was John's aunt. Both homes were located near the high school. In March 2010 our forty-forth president, Barack Obama, gave a speech on Health Care Reform on his one-hundredth day in office to a selected few hundred people at this very school. The high school had moved there in 1918, to what had been the old St. Charles Military Academy. A fire destroyed the original high school, which was then located on the eastern side of town.

Her house was similar to John's family home that he had grown up in.

The house was painted all white and looked a lot like John's house, from the front porch steps to the brick columns and covered porch. It had a small window in the front gable. And it also had a small glassed in porch that had been built onto the back of the house.

Built in the 1940s, it was quite a bit larger, and instead of only having an attic room, the entire upstairs was unfinished. It did have a regular floor just like many of the old homes had. The attic had even been partitioned off at some point in time, and as I recall, there was even electric wiring that ran through the studs up there too. There was even a real staircase that led up to it. I guess John's uncle had plans to finish the upstairs but just never did.

The house had much larger rooms. The living room, or parlor, if you will, had lots of floor-to-ceiling windows that were dressed up with romantic white lace curtains. Built-in bookcases and wooden columns flanked the archway leading into the formal dining room and a swinging door led into the kitchen and hall. Three bedrooms were located on the main level off a common hallway. Also located off the hallway, was the door to the staircase which led to the unfinished attic that had a tendency to open by itself.

But the two homes did have some striking similarities, right down to their inhabitants.

Just like John's other rental house, it too was occupied even when it was supposed to be vacant, if you know what I mean but in a much nicer sense.

One chilly spring day, I asked a maintenance man to take a look at the furnace because the housekeepers had reported that the house seemed cold. All the while they had been there sprucing it up, getting it ready for new tenants.

There was something about the air pressure in this home, though, that I had always noticed.

It could be one hundred degrees outside, and it would still be cool in this house. You see, the house had no air conditioning, not even a window air conditioner.

In fact, whenever a prospective tenant would become apprehensive after my telling them that the house had no AC, I would just explain that the house always seemed cool, even in extremely warm temperatures.

But it was cool outside that day, so maybe the furnace wasn't working after all, I thought.

Dale, a retired gentleman, was a stout middle-aged man and was beginning to gray at the temples. He worked as a maintenance man, doing odd jobs part-time for my company. He always had a joke or two to tell that he had heard at the local coffee shop.

But the story I'm going to tell you is certainly no joke.

Dale was in the basement looking at the furnace, when he heard a woman's voice.

Thinking that the woman was a real estate agent that had come to show the house, he climbed up the stairs from the basement. He thought he had better let her know that he was working in the basement. He didn't want to startle her.

But no one was there.

So he went back downstairs and began to tinker with the furnace.

Again, he heard a woman's voice. But this time, she was singing.

"Boy, she really has a beautiful voice," he thought.

He climbed back up the basement stairs again. No one was there.

Yet, another story I heard long ago when Dale first began doing odd jobs around the office,

It was a gorgeous summer day, and he was working inside of the glassed-in porch. The porch was located on the rear of the house just off the kitchen.

He heard singing coming from between the two houses.

"The voice was absolutely beautiful," he thought. "I've got to go see who it is and tell her just how beautiful she sounds."

He put his hammer down and walked outside and down the stairs from the glassed porch.

As soon as he rounded the back corner of the house, the singing suddenly stopped.

He thought to himself, "That's strange, she was there just a minute ago."

Once he was back on the porch, he began to hammer again. As soon as he stopped hammering, he heard the lovely voice again.

"This is crazy! I've got to see who this is!"

He hurried back around the corner again. Once again, the voice silenced immediately!

With that, he packed up his tools and came straight to my office to pay me a visit.

I was talking on the phone when he came in and sat down in front of me.

He just stared at me intently until I hung up the phone.

"Is everything okay?" I asked.

"I'm not finished over at the house yet," he explained. "The damnedest thing just happened over there. I was working out on the back porch and I heard singing, but every time I went to see who it was, the singing stopped! Have you ever had anything like that happen to you at that house? Has anybody else ever said anything?" he asked.

"No, I've never heard of anything like that happening before," I replied. "But it sounds to me like someone or something was trying to flirt with you," I playfully said and then laughed.

Then in the fall of '92, a couple in their late twenties with three young children rented the house.

They loved the high ceilings, all the big windows and hardwood floors, and even though the upstairs wasn't finished, it had plenty of room for their family.

Shortly after ringing in the New Year, I received a frantic call one afternoon from the fire department.

"Do you manage a house by the high school?"

"Yes, I do."

"You should come right away, it's on fire!"

I immediately hung up the phone and hurried over to the house.

As I drove down the street, I could see emergency vehicles lining the street and smoke filled the air.

There was no place to park for all the emergency vehicles, fire trucks, and the high school students' cars.

So I drove down one of the side streets and walked a block or so back to the house.

As I crossed the street, the tenant met me on the sidewalk. He was wearing his wife's pink bathrobe, and he was covered in soot. I guess he just grabbed the first thing that he could find to throw on his back, took the kids, and ran right out of the house.

Almost immediately, he began to blame me for the fire!

"You should have gotten that light switch fixed!" he shouted. "We don't have any insurance and now we've lost everything because you didn't get the electrical problems in the house fixed!"

Dumbfounded, I said, "What?" What are you talking about? You never called me about any electrical problem!"

Then the fire chief asked, "Are you the manager?"

"Yes, I am!"

"You need to get the right house numbers on this house," he shouted. "The damage wouldn't have been as bad if the house would have had the right numbers! The pumper had trouble finding the house!"

Everyone was shouting and pointing their fingers at me and I hadn't done anything!

First of all, and I have no idea why, but the addresses of the two rental houses were several digits apart! The houses were right next door to one another!

Second of all, in his next breath after scolding me about the address, the fire chief said that there had been no electrical problem. They had already figured out how the fire had started and it was pretty obvious.

"He's just trying to blame someone other than himself for the fire," the chief said. "The guy was taking a nap on the living room sofa, and the kids snuck off with his cigarette lighter. They were playing under the bed with it and caught the mattress on fire."

"Oh my god! Are the kids okay?" I asked.

"Yeah, they got scared, woke up their dad, and got him out of the house."

I was just sick over it.

When I was finally allowed to go inside of the house, I was shocked at what I saw.

Not so much that the fire had damaged the house. The firemen had quickly extinguished the blazing mattress and tossed it outside.

It was all the smoke and water damage that I just could not believe!

All the walls in the house were just black, from the smoke, and the scent of charred wood filled the air.

The once beautiful and romantic white lace curtains that covered the tall living room windows looked like black clouds whipping back and forth in the breeze that was coming through the open windows.

The wooden living room and dining room floors were so buckled that they just rolled like waves.

In the bedroom where the fire had started, there was a huge hole in the plaster ceiling that went through the floor of the attic and out through the roof! When I looked up, I could actually see the blue sky from inside of the bedroom and wet insulation and plaster covered the floor.

The burned mattress had been thrown into the backyard by the firemen.

It angered me that the tenant had tried to blame me for the fire, but I was ever so glad that no one had been hurt, especially his kids.

Now I was faced with the monumental task of the long and extensive renovation that lay ahead of me.

I began interviewing contractors and reviewing their bids. After narrowing the bids down to only three, I sent them off to the owner for his final approval.

By mid-February we had our building permit from the city, and by August all the work was completed and the house once again was approved for occupancy.

Yes, it was six months before things were back in order.

Many of the damaged walls had to be replastered.

The tall baseboards and window trim had to be especially made and the stain perfectly matched. Even the damaged doors had to be fabricated to match the old undamaged ones.

Much of the original hardwood flooring had to be taken up and new wood floors installed.

The old lighting fixtures were swapped with close replicas and some of the old wiring replaced.

John wanted the house to look just like it had before the fire. And so, everything had to look as much like the original as it possibly could.

It was August and the construction foreman contacted me to say that the house was ready for its final walk-through."

When I arrived, there were a couple of pickup trucks parked in the side yard with construction guys sprawled on the tailgates, just having a few beers at the end of the day after a job well done.

I had tried to stay out of their way during construction, except for an occasional visit now and then, whenever the foreman needed my approval for the right window trim or door casing. We were trying to make things look as original in the old house as we possibly could.

I walked up the front porch steps and into the front door and stopped just inside the living room.

It was breathtaking!

Just beautiful!

All the wooden floors had been replaced and they were gorgeous. The wide baseboards, window trim, and panel doors had been replaced, and everything just gleamed!

I was very pleased, to say the least.

"Where do I sign! The place looks fantastic! You guys did a phenomenal job!"

I was getting into my car when one of the construction guys hopped down from the tailgate of his pickup. "Ma'am . . . Can I talk to you for a minute?"

I was about to find out that the house had actually been occupied the whole time.

Very tall and in his midtwenties, I'd say. Kind of cute, with messy and sandy-colored hair. Dressed in dirty white overalls and work boots, he took a couple steps toward me.

"Sure, what is it?" I asked, stepping back out of the street and onto the sidewalk.

"Well . . ." He hesitated and the other guys snickered.

"Has anybody ever said anything about weird stuff happening here?"

Pretending to be unsuspecting, I answered, "No! Like what?"

The other guys laughed again.

Then he began to tell his story.

"A couple weeks ago, we were getting close to our deadline. So I was here, working by myself, late at night."

There I went again, goose bumps, chills, and tears.

"I was working in the bathroom and I hear something fall on the floor in the other room. A circular saw had fallen off the workbench we had set up in the dining room. So I cleared a spot for it in the middle of the bench, picked the saw up off the floor, and went back to work. I was only in the bathroom a few minutes and I heard it fall again!"

By now, this guy was killing me. I had to fight the tears back, trying not to let on that I actually did know a thing or two about the house. And the other guys weren't laughing anymore either.

Had they had an experience or two of their own but were just too "macho" to admit it?

He went on to explain, "When I heard the saw fall on the floor again, I didn't turn off any lights. I left all the lights in the house on that night, and I didn't even stop to lock the door! But when I was going out the back door, I glanced through the kitchen and into the dining room and the saw was on the floor again!"

"Really!"

Then I confessed.

"Well, one of the maintenance men reported that he had heard a woman singing, but when he went to look for her, the singing stopped."

With wide eyes, two of the other guys just looked at one another.

I looked at them and said, "Why? Did you guys hear or see something?"

They both shook their heads and said no, but I think they probably did know something and were just too macho to admit it.

After all, how many tailgating, beer-drinking kind of guys would admit to such a thing.

But here's an interesting point.

It wasn't until I was writing "The Attic Room" that it came to me some fifteen years later.

No woman had ever reported having any unusual experience in the home except that the house felt cool even in one-hundred-degree weather. Even I experienced that feeling. It was only the men who reported the strange goings on.

It would seem to me that these men were being "'flirted" with.

Now, I ask you, who would tell such stories if they hadn't taken place?

Before John sold the house, there were four more occupants to live in the house after the fire.

The first to move in to the newly renovated home were Jerry and Deanna, a younger couple who lived there for two years.

On the first day of the month, Jerry had come in to my office to pay his rent. As he handed the rent check to me, he said, "The strangest thing happened to me."

"Here we go again," I thought.

"I put Christmas lights up on the house and the strangest thing happened. I put up blue lights and the first night they were blue. But the second night when I turned them on, they were red!"

"Do you think something could be wrong with the power coming in to the house?" he asked.

"Gee, I don't know. I guess there could be."

But you know what I was really thinking.

Then the summer of '95, Jerry was arrested for reasons I do not know.

What I do know is that, while Jerry was behind bars, he and his wife were conspiring via the telephone, to do harm to the prosecuting attorney.

Deanna too was then arrested on conspiracy charges.

Well, needless to say, Jerry and Deanna were asked to move out!

Then there was Billy, a single man who only lived in the house for one year and never reported any disturbances. But really. A single man? If the truth were to be told, I'm sure he had his fair share of "flirtations" too.

Which brings me to Tina, a young single woman that lived happily in the house for five long years! She really didn't want to move, either. In fact, she wanted to buy the house, but much to her dismay, she could not afford John's asking price.

And so, yet another couple purchased the house. They poured a lot of money into finishing the upstairs, but then sold it just one year later.

Why would they sell it so quickly?

And they sold it, to none other than . . . ?

Yes, a single woman.

But then just a few years later even she moved out of the house and the house became a rental once again.

I was having breakfast at the little diner near the old house on a cold winter morning just after New Year's Day. Looking out the window of the diner, there it was. A sign staked in the front yard of the old house: "For Rent."

Of course, I wondered why.

Then early that spring, an old client contacted me to lease another one of his homes that I never knew that he had owned. He and his wife had been managing this property themselves for the past forty years where a small family lived until one of the family members passed on.

As I pulled up in front of the house, I realized that it was the very same place that I had parked my car on the day of the fire at the house by the school.

I had just put the "For Lease" sign in the window and was on the tiny front porch locking up when, I noticed that a small boxy-looking car had stopped at the corner. It was a Kia Soul—no pun intended.

A young woman with her light brown hair pulled back in a ponytail exited the car from the passenger door. Standing in the middle of the street she yelled, "How much are you asking for rent? Do you have the time to show it to me? I just live right there in that big white house." She pointed to the old house I had managed for years.

Then I pointed to the house. "That white house?" As you can imagine, I was excited to talk to someone about the house!

Almost immediately she said, "We just moved in at the first of the year and we hate it!"

"Why do you hate it?" I asked. "I managed that house for the previous owner for fifteen years."

"I don't know, we just hate it . . . That house is crazy."

Well, that was the first time I had ever heard anyone call the house crazy.

Pressing for more information, I asked, "What do you mean crazy?"

"Oh, I don't know, we just hate living there and we've just got to get out. Separated from my husband, I rented the house for me and my girls. But soon after we moved into the house, my husband began staying with us a few days a week and . . ." The young woman hesitated. "We just don't like living there." And once again she said, "That house is crazy!"

Having heard so many of the stories through the years, I was just dying to know what "crazy" meant.

"Crazy? What do you mean by crazy?" I pressed for more information.

She explained, "The utility bills are high . . . I don't know, the house is just crazy!" After only two months of paying the utility bills, how could she possibly make the assumption that the bills were high? No one ever complained to me in fifteen years about the high cost of the utilities. Tenants complained to me about strange happenings, but never once about the utilities being high.

I'm certain the young woman was just afraid to share her secrets about the house with me, fearing I would think that *she* was crazy!

It seemed that all was well until the woman's husband entered the picture.

I think it to be very strange that only the women seem to be comfortable in this home, and yet it's the men that were uncomfortable.

Is it because of the Flirtatious One?

Also located off the hallway was the door to the staircase that led to the unfinished attic that had a tendency to open by itself.

While attending a writing class, the instructor asked everyone to pick one character in the book that they were writing and create one page to describe them. I had heard so many stories from various tenants about John's family homes. Especially that "White Story and a Half" near the old Military Academy, a.k.a. the old St. Charles High School. I decided to choose the Flirtatious One because I almost felt like I knew her, at least good enough to imagine how she may have appeared as well as her feelings toward men, and so without further ado, I give you . . .

The Painted Lady

Her existence was experienced by that of men.

Her short wavy hair was dark, she had a lock of curled hair, and a painted beauty mark on her porcelain white cheek.

With her hourglass shape, she wore a red-lace corset trimmed in shiny black silk and a tiny red bow adorned the plunging lines between her breast.

Her laced-up high heels, dark, hosiery and black garter accentuated her long slender legs.

Do you see her?

She has roamed the rooms of that old house, just to be near what was once the old Military Academy.

Her existence was felt by men, yet her presence went unnoticed by that of women.

Playfully she would tease the mortal man by making something fall from a shelf. She could be heard with a song, intriguing him with her beautiful voice that would suddenly silence whenever his curiosity peaked with the urge to seek her.

Men feared her though she longed for their company, but her unexplained antics only drove them away for fear of the unknown.

She's the Flirtatious One.

Did you think that was weird? My instructor did! LOL.

Haunted Caravan

Part 1

Twilight Zone

Caravan, or some may call it house tour. Is just something that Realtors do.

Usually about once a week or so, real estate agents pile into cars and caravan around the countryside. We drive around, looking at all the newly listed properties for sale that one agent or another in the office had signed up just the week before to market and sell.

For years, I could never understand why on caravan I occasionally felt sick!

Not until one day after touring one of the new listings—and no, I was not carsick either.

I just happened to sit next to Shirley. She was already in the car sitting in the back seat.

Shirley was quite a bit older than me. She was a full-figured gal with short graying hair and had a very pretty face. If fact, she was beautiful inside and out. Shirley had a great sense of humor too and was just as nice a person could ever be.

"Why, Nan, you're as white as a sheet," she said. "You look like you've just seen a ghost! What's wrong? Are you okay?"

"No, not really. I feel cold and sweaty. Sick to my stomach and feel like I'm going to pass out."

"When did you start to feel sick?" she asked. "You seemed fine when we were on the porch waiting for David to unlock the front door."

We were standing on the front porch of David's new listing located on the easternmost side of town, just a few blocks away from the river.

Built at the turn of the century in 1925, the house was situated on a nice level lot and sat very close to the street. It looked just like a gingerbread house, except it was a little over 1,900 square feet. A bit large for a gingerbread house, I'd say. Three steps led up to the old front porch covered in several layers of gray paint. The porch railings had two by two slats for spindles and white four by four posts supported the porch roof.

We were all laughing and talking as we shuffled into the vacant house. We scattered as we usually did whenever we knew that a house wasn't occupied by anyone (well, we thought it wasn't occupied).

Some of the ladies went to view the kitchen, and of course, the men just headed straight for the basement and a handful of us headed up the stairs, as I did.

Being the last to go up the wooden staircase, as I stood in the hallway at the top of the stairs, I glanced to my right and realized there was a second staircase. I imagined that it led to the kitchen, but I never got a chance to check it out.

In fact, I never made it any further than the top of that staircase.

Standing there alone, as I studied the second staircase, imagining that it led back down to what I thought to be the kitchen, all of a sudden it hit me.

It was as if something went right through me. I began to sweat, yet I was freezing cold. I felt like I was going to vomit and pass out all at the same time.

Feeling weak and sick to my stomach, I made it back down the stairs. Clutching the hand railing, I noticed that it had been worn smooth over the years.

Then I was out the front door and down the wooden front porch steps with shaky legs, walking as fast as I possibly could in heels.

I climbed into the first car that was parked right in front of the house and sat beside Shirley.

After she heard what had happened to me, she began to explain. ""You're just sensitive is all. To spirits."

"You know, don't you?"

Shirley was also very religious.

I thought, "Wow, I can't believe she's telling me all these things."

"They sense that about you. That you're sensitive to them, and they just want to be with you because you're alive and they miss that feeling."

"Oh, great, now I have spirits that want to be with me?"

"You've got to be kidding me," I thought.

I still didn't feel very well and so I just sat and listened to her talk.

As did everyone else in the car!

After that day, I became known around the office for my paranormal experiences.

Then several years later on Halloween night, my husband's mother, Anna Mae, stopped by our house. She had brought treats for her grandkids as she always did on every holiday or occasion.

"Too bad my ankle's sore or I'd take you kids to a haunted house!" she joked.

The kids loved to go to haunted houses.

And since I would never, never be "caught dead" in one, my best friend Jo, who also loved going to haunted houses, would usually pick the kids up and take them to a haunted house for a good scare on Halloween night.

"Yeah, let's go to a haunted house!" the kids all shouted as they looked at me.

"Don't look at me. No way!" I exclaimed. "I've had my share of real haunted houses, and I'm not about to set foot inside any place that even resembles a haunted house."

Puzzled, my mother-in-law looked at me and asked, "What did you mean by that?"

"Oh, over the years, I've just had my share of experiences in some of the houses that I've either managed as a rental house or toured on caravan."

"What kind of experiences?" she asked.

"Mom, tell grandma some of your ghost stories!" the kids screamed.

They were so excited, they forgot all about going to a haunted house.

It seemed like a fitting thing to do on a Halloween night. So we turned the lights down low and lit some candles, and I began to tell my ghost stories.

But when I started to tell the story about the "gingerbread" house, Anna Mae became very inquisitive.

"Where was the house at? On the left side of the street or on the right? Was it the first? Or was it the second house on the left?"

Anna Mae had spent her teenage years growing up on that very street and in later years as a young bride. She lived just a few doors down, waiting for her new husband, Sammy, to return home from the World War II and knew the neighborhood.

"Do you know the house?" I asked.

She pondered her thoughts for a moment.

As the flicker of the candles danced across her face, everyone stared at her intently just waiting for her to say something. The look on her face was . . . you know, the look someone gets when they want to tell you something but aren't sure if they should.

"Yes," Anna Mae said softly.

Then she tilted her head and quietly said, "That was Mrs. Diermann's house. Grace Diermann."

"The Diermanns lived in the second house on the left."

Then a sorrowful look came over her and she began nodding her head.

"Grace was so distraught and beside herself after losing her husband to the war . . ."

"What? What happened?" I asked.

Grandma wasn't too sure if she should say anything in front of the kids.

Calmly Anna Mae looked at Jude and me.

She leaned a little closer to us.

Then she whispered softly, "She hung herself in the stairway."

Just then, goose bumps and chills came over me!

I shuddered to think when I looked at the stairway that led to the kitchen and the sick feeling that came over me.

Could it have been Mrs. Diermann?

Just then, I felt like we were in the middle of a *Twilight Zone* rerun.

Do-do-do-do-do, do-do-do-do . . .

Haunted Caravan

Part 2

Her Imaginary Friend

Then there was my visit to the very first hospital in town. It had been established in the late 1800s. It was opened by the Sisters of St. Mary in 1885.

What on earth would ever make me think that I could ever tour this property without an incident is beyond me!

What was I thinking?

I had heard that this particular building was built of several levels. But when we drove up in front of it, it just looked like a normal 1.5-story building.

I soon learned that a few of the buildings many floors were located below ground level.

It didn't resemble a hospital at all. In fact, over the years, one of the old buildings many owners had covered the old bricks up with stucco. And it had even been painted a medium blue color.

Once inside everyone scattered, and I found myself alone once again.

But without a care, I began to explore the old building.

I wandered through every level, eventually ending up on the fifth level.

Or would it have been the first level?

Anyway, there I was on the bottom level of the building with nothing much to see except one single room.

The door was standing open, and so I just moseyed around the corner and on into the room.

It was a strange little room, about eleven feet by twelve feet in size.

There wasn't anything odd about that, but there certainly was something strange about this particular room.

Made of cement, there was a five-foot area in the center of the room that was divided by a curb, so to speak. The curb was on each side of the room, and it ran the entire length and with about three feet to the wall on either side. On the opposite side of the room, there was one step up that led to a door. The door was closed.

"What a weird little room," I thought. "I wonder what this room was used for back in the day." (It wasn't until 2016 when I began to watch HBO's *Six Feet Under* reruns that I realized what that room was probably used for.)

I was curious as to what was behind the closed door on the opposite end of the room.

I started to walk across the room and then it hit me! I felt nauseous. Cold but sweaty. And that feeling! Like I was going to pass right out.

I became disoriented.

I had not paid any attention to how I had even gotten to that room on the bottom level of the property.

I just began climbing stairs and going down hallways until finally I found the rear entrance to the building and made my way out to the backyard.

I sat down on an old tree stump to collect myself for a moment. Then I wandered around to the front of the building, just like nothing had ever happened. The other agents were beginning to get into the cars, and I gladly followed! No one asked if anything was wrong, and I didn't say a word about what had just happened. Don't ask? Don't tell!

Later that day after house tour, I rushed to my mother's house to pick up my daughter. I was in a hurry to drive her to kindergarten class.

My daughter, Karie, who was five at the time, was with my mother, Eileen.

My mom always watched our daughter before school every day.

Karie and I had driven about a half a mile down the road when she began saying things to me like, "Mom, let my friend in. Let my friend in!"

I looked at her in the rearview mirror.

She was looking outside the car window.

"What!" I shouted. She was scaring me.

"Stop the car. Let my friend in!"

"Karie, be quiet, there is no one outside of the car."

"Yes, there is. Please stop the car, Mommy!"

Freaked out, I hurried and hit the button to the power windows to roll them up.

Karie really upset me that day. She really had me going!

You see, at the age of, five she had never, ever, absolutely not ever have an imaginary friend in her life—except that one day.

And she never had an imaginary friend ever again.

Haunted Caravan

Part 3

Age Really Doesn't Matter

It seemed like it would be just another ordinary day. The houses on the caravan list were just a few newer ranch-style homes. Nothing to worry about, a piece of cake.

Was I ever wrong!

As we drove up to the house, I realized that it was one that I happened to have driven by on my way to and from the office.

You know that old saying "Age doesn't matter"?

The home was just ten to fifteen years old. It was an L-shaped ranch with a big front porch and white pillars, a brick front with black shutters, and a long curvy driveway. I recognized the house, but I had never recalled ever seeing anyone there. Not even a car in the driveway and I drove past it every day.

The front door opened into a large entry foyer and straight ahead was the cozy family room. The home was nicely furnished, but it was a bit dated. Just to the right of the foyer was the formal dining room, which was where I began my tour of the house.

I strolled through the dining room and took notice of the pretty cherry-wood dining room table and into the adjoining kitchen with lots of maple cabinets. Then passing through the family room, I glanced into the backyard through the windows that flanked both sides of the wood-burning fireplace made of red brick. I then found myself in the hallway where the bedrooms were located.

The master bedroom seemed to be a decent size and was beautifully decorated, I thought to myself as I passed by the doorway.

The next room appeared to be the bedroom of a small child. A bright red tricycle was parked in the middle of the room.

But the very instant that I laid my eyes on the little red tricycle, that old feeling went straight through me again!

I didn't know if I would make it outside, but I headed for the front door as fast as I could.

Once outside, there was nowhere to sit down, and so I leaned against the bumper of my manager's van.

I'm a car buff at heart and would not want anyone leaning on my car. But feeling as though I would pass out, I had no choice but to have a seat on the bumper of Robert's van.

Robert, my manager at that time and co-owner of the company with his brother, Donald, spotted me sitting on the bumper of his van.

A middle-aged man with thinning sandy blond hair, Robert was walking toward me with a funny smirk on his face.

"What are you doing sitting out here all by yourself?" he asked.

"Oh, I just don't feel all that great today."

He began to laugh at me.

"Oh, come on!" he kidded. "You can't tell me that you don't know."

Still not feeling well, I didn't feel like playing whatever guessing game Robert wanted to play.

I just shook my head no.

"You really don't know, do you? You haven't heard anyone in the office talk about this house?"

"No!" I said, wishing he would just let me be.

About that time, most of the other agents were coming out of the front door.

Robert turned and said to them, "Hey, Nancy says she doesn't know anything about the family that lived here!"

"Oh, sure she doesn't." Joseph laughed.

Evidently, I was the last to know that the people that lived in the house never returned home from their family vacation.

They were a family of five who died in a car crash while vacationing out west.

It had taken the heirs several years to get the family's affairs in order before they were able to sell the house.

I was saddened to think about it, especially when I thought about the little red tricycle sitting in the middle of the little boy's room.

A few weeks passed by and Robert came to my office and stood in the doorway.

He seemed a bit embarrassed by whatever it was that he was about to ask me.

"I don't know if you would be interested in doing this or not, but the tenants in my six-family building hear things at night. The tenants claim that it sounds like a lot of people screaming and fighting but there's never anyone there."

"Now, where have I heard this before?" I thought to myself.

"So the story I've heard is that my apartment building is built on the grounds of an Indian fight—"

"You can just stop right there, Robert! No way! There is no way that I am going to go there!"

After all, this was not something that I particularly enjoyed, was proud of, wanted, or ever expected to happen.

Imagine yourself.

You know the feeling.

You feel lightheaded, sick to your stomach, then you break out into a cold sweat.

Why would you want to go looking for something that makes you feel that way?

"Sorry, but there's no way!" I said firmly.

Robert laughed and shrugged his shoulders.

"Well, I didn't think you would, but I just thought I'd ask."

I guess I had proven a point that day on caravan. Maybe spirits really did exist after all.

The very fact that a co-owner of the company asked for my help made me realize that my point had been taken.

I asked him, "So I guess you might believe just a little that maybe I really do sense 'things'?"

His reply was none other than "Point taken."

Now here's another interesting point.

Remember the story "The Attic Room"?

And when the newspaper reporter interviewed one of the homeowners?

The homeowner replied, "The house is too young to be haunted, it's only sixty-five years old. So give me a break."

Maybe the age really doesn't matter.

That Old House

He opened the door of the old house that he had just won the bid on at a foreclosure sale, knowing him, most likely having used a credit card to get inside. He gasps, "Good God!"

Some twenty-five years earlier, back in the '70s, Jude and I were a newly married young couple. His sweet Grandma Jones offered us just to take over the payments on one of her rental properties, and we could own our very first home.

When my new husband, Jude, took me to see the little four-room house with pink siding, I begged him just to rent us a nice apartment. "I'm not living there, I'll just stay at my parents' house, and you can just live with yours."

Okay, maybe I was a little stuck-up, but I was used to all the comforts of home. Little things. You know, like a real furnace to keep warm and maybe a shower. The little house had a wall furnace and only a baby blue tub and a few homemade kitchen cabinets made of plywood. They were painted an ivory color and had a tiny little bouquet of multicolored flowers painted in the center of each cabinet door.

So with me refusing to move in to the little house and my husband refusing to rent an apartment, my dad, Kenny, stepped up. He and Jude spent nearly every night and weekend at the house fixing it up. After six long months, we were ready to move in to our newly renovated home.

Being the first in our circle of friends to have a place of our own, it quickly became the go to place for them to hang out.

It was fight night, and the guys were coming over to watch a boxing match on TV. We girls decided to go cruising around town so, we grabbed a few beers and all piled in to my '70 Dodge Dart Swinger. We hadn't been out for very long. In fact, we hadn't even made it out of the neighborhood when I pulled up behind an old car that was just sitting at the Stop sign. Through the rear window of the car ahead of us, we could see someone inside with their head down, like they were resting it on the steering wheel. Not knowing what else to do, I honked the horn a couple times. With that, the person jerked their head up, and the next thing we knew, the car's reverse lights came on and the rear of the car ahead of us came smashing into the front of my car! The steam from the damaged radiator rose up into the air, and the car sped away. I quickly riffled through my purse for something to write the license plate number down, C2B006. People from neighboring houses had heard the crash and came running out to tell us the police were already on their way. "This is great," I thought. There were a bunch of underage girls with beer in the car, and the police were on their way. The cool thing about those cars from the early '70s is that some of them had these really big air vents near the floorboard. It's like you could just open the little door of the vent, and believe it or not, the vent could hold a six-pack. So my car got towed, and fight night was ruined for the guys having to retrieve us from the side of the road and the police call to say they'd caught the guy and wanted me to identify him.

"We're sending a car to pick you up."

"But, Officer, I never saw his face."

About that time, a patrol car rolled up in front of the house. "Now, we have the suspect waiting in another car up at the school. All we are going to do is shine our headlights into the car so you can try to ID him."

"But I'm telling you—I never saw his face."

So we pulled onto the school parking lot, and this guy was jumping around all over the back seat of the other patrol car. His eyes were crazy. He had long dark curly hair, was sweating profusely, and was making faces at us through the car window. The officer said, "His name is Renny and he's higher than a kite. He was driving a stolen car through some backyards down off Elm Street in the Runnymeade neighborhood. Recognize 'im?"

"Nope, I keep saying that I never saw his face. Not until just now."

If it wasn't bad enough that my car got bashed in and fight night got ruined, we had to claim the damage to the car on our insurance under the uninsured motorist clause due to the car having been stolen! Thanks a lot, Renny, the story made the newspaper, and your crazy eyes along with license plate number C2B006 will forever be engrained in my memory.

Then one evening, having ran out of firewood for the wood-burning stove that we had installed to help heat the house, I just happened to have one of those fire logs made of wax and saw dust handy. Friends were over and everyone wanted to keep the fire going, so I decided to put this log on the fire. "DO NOT ADD TO AN EXISTING FIRE," the packaging read, but the package didn't say what would happen if the log were added to a fire that was already going. So despite advice from friends and family and I being young and dumb, I went ahead and tossed it into the cast iron stove. Almost immediately the wax and sawdust log burst into flames, and soon the flames were up inside the flue and dancing out of the hole where the little lever for the damper came through the pipe. Soon sparks were flying out of the chimney and all over the roof. Needless to say, the party was over when the fire truck arrived with its lights spinning and flashing and sirens blaring.

Not long after *my* flue fire, we were telling friends the story of how we were expecting our daughter and were going to buy this antique rocking chair at the old auction house on Highway 94 North. Our friend Bryan was rocking in the chair as we told of how we had lost the bid on the chair and of how Jude had found the buyer after the auction had ended and offered the guy more money for the chair. Still talking about the chair, Bryan got up to grab another beer from the fridge, came back in to the living room, and sat back down in the rocking chair, and the seat broke into three pieces right under him! LOL. I can still see that priceless look on Bryan's face. Some thirty-odd years later, I still have the rocker. I couldn't sell it at a garage sale, not online either. Even our kids wouldn't take it when their kids were born. Guess I'm just stuck with it. I do use it once a year at Christmastime to read "'Twas the night before Christmas" to our eight grandkids, all the while giving them clues of where their gifts might be found, and then they would run off through the house to find them. The rocker just sat in one corner of my room, but recently I wanted to snap a pic of it for this story. So I moved it into my home office for its photo shoot, then I moved it back to the corner in my bedroom. That night, I woke up in the middle of the night and I could hear the rocking chair making subtle creaking noises here and there. I wasn't about to open my eyes to look at it and told myself, "It's just old wood, and when I moved it from room to room, it just had to settle itself back down again, that's all." I rolled over and went back to sleep, thinking to myself, *Creepy old chair.*

There were other weird things that happened at that old house too. Just about every evening while watching TV, out of the corner of my eye, I would catch a glimpse of a whitish cloudlike apparition float from the bathroom, which was located in the hallway, and it would disappear into the master bedroom. At the time, I had never even thought about a house being haunted. Up until that time in my life, I had only ever been afraid of the boogeyman that always lived in my parents' basement. But now, I'm not so sure that our first home wasn't haunted! Talking about it now, Jude will even admit to seeing that floating apparition.

How about that long night when every time we were just about to fall asleep and Jude Jr. would let out this bone-chilling scream from his bedroom. We'd both jump up out of bed and run to his room. Jude Jr.'s sitting up in bed with his covers pulled up to his chin, pointing his little shaking finger at the closet, terrified with tears streaming down his cheeks. "Cats! Cats in my closet!"

We'd turn on the lights and tell him, "See, there aren't any cats in your closet. Go back to sleep now." Drifting back off to sleep and we would hear, "Aaahhhhhhhhh!" Jude Jr.'s bloodcurdling screams again and again. It seemed like it went on all night long. After a while, even we began to freak out and started to believe that maybe there were really cats in the closet. I don't think any of us slept at all that night.

We did have a couple cats, but they were outdoor cats that, even on freezing cold snowy nights, would never come inside the house. We were finishing up dinner one night, and our neighbor

Mike knocked on the door. "One of your cats just got hit by a car and it's in the road. I think it's dead."

There we were standing in the front yard, talking about getting a shovel to bury it and looking at the cat lying in the middle of the street motionless. All of a sudden, this cat jumped up and took off running like a bat out a hell. Mike, Jude, and I just looked at each other and laughed. Nine lives?

By now, it's the late '70s and the real estate market was booming. New construction was everywhere you looked, even in the middle of our old neighborhood. Little did we know just how much trouble that it was going to cause our little house.

Unbeknownst to us, the plans for the new subdivision being built up the street from our house didn't include a good drainage system for watershed. That old saying "When it rains, it pours"?

When it rained, it poured. When it poured, the muddy water flowed through all the yards that were below the new development. Eventually the rushing water formed ditches, and all sorts of things would float down them like coolers, trash, and tree limbs. You name it, and it floated right through our yard. We went to all the city council meetings and begged for help, arguing that our situation was the city's fault, but our pleas for help only fell on deaf ears.

Lightning, thunder, and torrential downpours came one evening—one evening that happened to be on the night of a city council meeting. Sitting on top of our kitchen table with my water-soaked feet on the seat of a kitchen chair, I watched the water running under the front door of our home and right out the back door. Jude had gone outside in the pouring rain to help a neighbor remove somebody's red Coleman cooler from the ditch. It had floated down the street and had become lodged and was damning up the flow of the water. Feeling hopeless, I pulled myself together, got in the car, and drove right down to the city hall.

Ninety-five pounds and soaking wet, before the city council, I begged for their mercy and explained what was happening to our property at that very moment. The city had made an enormous mistake in approving the developers' plans for the new subdivision. One of the council members asked what made me think that it was the council's fault, and I began to explain, "You approved a plan that allowed the developer of the new subdivision in my neighborhood to shed water from the streets on to our properties and it's flooding our houses!"

"Yeah, and rain falls from the sky too." He laughed. Other members of the city council began to laugh, and even citizens waiting for their turn to address the council with their own concerns laughed at the jerk too. I burst into tears and left the council chambers.

Catching up with me out in the hallway, our councilman tried to calm me by telling me, "Don't worry," said Mr. Kelly, "I'll make the other members see what we're talking about."

After that rainy night, a little progress was made. Mr. Kelly organized a little field trip to our property for the council members, showing them where the storm water sewer pipes from the newly built subdivision discharged and walking what was now more of a creek than a ditch. Some of the men stood on our driveway, shaking their heads and apologizing.

Of course, there were always those who agree to disagree, and we just weren't able to get enough votes to get the approval to fix the problem. Finally, we found a local attorney. He must have felt sorry for us and took our case pro bono. Between this generous man and our diligent councilman, we were able to get enough funds through community development to get the storm sewers we so desperately needed.

The damage was done. Our house now had termites. They just love old damp wood and deteriorating floor joist. The next few years were spent fixing the old house up, replacing floor joists and wall studs, and even adding a new master bedroom and two car garage.

We were excited, but the new addition was no picnic either and seemed it was doomed right from the start!

The so-called contractor that we had hired only worked a day or two and then disappeared with our down payment money. He was nowhere to be found and had left his dump truck parked in the yard, smack dab right in the middle of where the addition was to be built. After weeks of calling the man and mailing him certified letters, we hired a new contractor and had the dump truck towed away.

Once the addition was complete, even getting a simple thing like a driveway poured became a monumental task. For days after the forms had been set for the new driveway, we left message after message for our concrete contractor. "The way you have the forms set up is not right. It's not how we want the driveway. The grade is going to be too steep. Please call us back so we can discuss it."

I ask you, would someone, anyone, please tell me why is it so hard to get people to return a phone call?

With none of our phone calls returned, I got home from the office and the concrete guy was just putting the finishing touches on our new very "steep" driveway. Before I even had a chance to turn off the engine, the guy was running to my car. He's flailing his arms around and shouting at me through the closed car window, "It's how your husband wants it, I know it's how he wanted it."

I got out of the car, shaking my head, and said sarcastically, "Nope, I don't think so." Storming past the guy, leaving him standing there in the street, I went into the house and slammed the door shut.

Now, about that driveway. This story will freak anyone out.

One snowy evening that winter, I arrived home from the office and parked on the driveway. Jude's on the front porch, talking to our friend Joe, who had just stopped by. Our son, Jason, with his arms crossed and his little chin resting on the windowsill, was staring out the picture window, just watching the snow coming down. Without saying a word, Joe pushed Jude out of the way and Jude's like, "What the?" Without a sound, my '76 Lemans had just quietly, slowly slid right down that steep driveway coming to rest with its front bumper only inches away from the window that Jason had been, still was looking out of it!

'Twas the night before Christmas, Jude had just laid down for a long winter's nap, and I was hanging Christmas lights. After plugging in the Christmas lights, I had hung in the picture window, and I went out to see how they looked. Standing there admiring my work of art, out of corner of my eye, I saw a man, a tall dark thin man in a long black trench coat and hat standing in front of the garage. I started to hyperventilate and run as fast as I could back inside the house. I tried to slam the front door closed. Over and over again, I tried to shut the door, but it just wouldn't close. Then I realized in a panic I had locked the deadbolt before trying to close the door. Finally, after getting the door closed and *then* locking it, I ran to the master bedroom where Jude was napping. I shook him but couldn't utter a sound. I was trying to talk, but the words just wouldn't come out. At last, I blurted out, "THERE'S A MAN OUTSIDE!" We both run out and on to the front porch, but no one's there. "He was just there, right there in front of the garage door," I shouted.

About that time, we heard banging on our back door, so we ran back inside to look out the window, and it's our elderly neighbor Mike dressed in nothing but his whitey-tighties. He was out of breath but managed to tell us that a man had just walked right into his back door. "I told him to get the hell out of my house, then I ran right over here!" We immediately call the police. The police finally came and the man in the hat and coat came out of the shadows with a stick in his hand, waving it around at them. Apparently, he was just as shaken up as we were. It turned out that a carload of kids had picked this elderly gentleman up from an assisted living facility in the Chesterfield Valley, had taken this poor old man for a joy ride, and then dropped him off at the edge of our town that just happened to be right where we lived! He had been reported missing, so when the police arrived, they knew exactly who the old guy was and where he belonged. Eventually, we decided that even the addition of the new room wouldn't be big enough for our growing family. So after nine let's just say eventful years, we decided to sell and move on.

But not too fast—it's not over yet!

Closing day. How exciting or so one would think? All our stuff was all packed up in boxes sitting in the garage. The moving truck was on the driveway waiting to take everything to our new home on the little lake I had found. Of course, we needed to close on our old house before we could close on the new home. Having never sold a house before, we nervously got to the title company, were anxious to sign the papers, and found that our nerves were not unfounded. Our buyer had not shown up for closing! Days went by before finally tracking the buyer down. He explained to me that he had just gotten bad news about his health and was no longer going to buy our house. After he hurt his leg on the job working for the railroad, his wound hadn't been taken care of properly and was diagnosed with gangrene. The man was going to lose his leg. "But the house would be perfect for you," I pleaded with the man. "Everything's all on one level, no steps."

The man said, "I don't care what you say, lady. I'm not buying your house!"

You can imagine our disappointment.

This may sound ridiculous, but as a Realtor, I've always been glad that it happened to me rather than a client. I can't imagine having to tell any of my sellers that the buyer of their house just didn't show up for closing. Worse yet, telling them they wouldn't be able to buy their new house either. We gave up on selling for another two years, but they say that everything happens for a reason. Ironically, two years later, we sold the old house for a few thousand dollars more and bought that very same house on the little lake for a few thousand dollars less.

But wait just a minute.

Some relative thought they should receive a cut out of what we had made on that old house. Really? After eleven years? After all our hard work, hard times, blood, sweat, and tears? No way!

Some thirteen years after selling our first little house, a colleague of mine who was off to a foreclosure sale stopped to ask me a few questions before rushing out the door. He questioned me about the little house I once owned. I did my best to discourage him from having anything to do with that old house. I talked as fast as I possibly could, trying to give as much information to him in the sixty seconds I had before he hurried out the door. But he had no time to listen to reason and didn't want to be late for the sale. "Oh, I'm not scared," he said as he walked out the door.

"Good God," he gasped as he swung the door open and saw the living room floor had fallen right through the floor joist of that old house.

To this day, I never do miss a chance to say, "I tried to tell you not to buy THAT OLD HOUSE."

An Unexpected Visitor

In August 2015 having spent thirteen days in the hospital with a collapsed lung, I was lucky to have a room with a view. Look closer at the Orb in the center of the woods, bring it closer using a computer or cell phone. Do you see the unexpected visitor? Perhaps the face of a dog or a fox?

Hauntingly Erie Possessions

The Little Snow Globe

Now here's a little ditty about the time I went to the bank to cash a few US Savings Bonds my dad had kept for me since I was a little girl.

After my dad passed away, I had gone to the bank with my savings bonds in hand to cash them in. After cashing the bonds, I walked to my car, opened the door and climbed in. Of course, there wasn't anything unusual about that, but when I shut the car door music began to play from my backseat!

♪ *We wish you a Merry Christmas, we wish you a Merry Christmas, we wish you a Merry Christmas and a Happy New Year* ♪…and the whole song played on.

I thought my eyes were going bug right out of my head!

I quickly got right back out of my car and removed the white plastic trash bag that was filled with donation items for the Goodwill store from my backseat. I sat the bag down on the banks parking lot and rifled through the bag until I finally found it, a holiday snow globe that I knew had not played in years! I repeatedly just kept on tipping it upside down, rocking it back and forth, I tapped on it and shook it up and down, just trying anything to get it to play again, but it just wouldn't play another note.

I decided that I couldn't part with the little snow globe after what had just happened. So, I held it up to the sky and simply said, "Thanks Dad"!

It's still on a shelf in my basement, all the water that was in it has now dissipated, leaving nothing in it but the tiny white snow balls that use to swirl around inside. I've never heard it play again, but I won't ever part with the little snow globe.

Those Old Boots

Every year I drag my husband to the Main Street Music Hall at the lake to see the new seasons show. Having arrived a bit early, we decided to peruse one of the quaint old gift shops near the music hall.

It was your usual touristy type store with wares like, souvenirs, Lake of the Ozark's tee shirts, little trinkets, jewelry, clothing and some antiques just to name a few.

Jude was just browsing around the store and I was checking out the shops small selection of antiques. There were toys, some old photographs and dishes, then there was this pair of women's vintage lace up boots. They were all dusty, just sitting there on the shelf, but the very moment I laid my eyes on them that old feeling went straight through me…cold, yet I was beginning to sweat, and I felt like I would vomit and pass out all at the same time. I hurried to the exit and out the door, but there was nowhere to sit down. So, I made my way to the dark storefront across the courtyard and found a small bench.

After looking all over the place for me, Jude finally found me just sitting out there on that bench. "What are you doing outside and all the way over here sitting in the dark"? "I was wondering where you disappeared to". "I turned around and you were gone"!

I explained, "there was this pair of a women's old boots, and when I looked at those old boots, it felt like they just went straight through me"!

"No way" Jude said, as he laughed at me.

He doesn't believe…do you?

Creepy Old Chair

Friends were visiting, and we were doing a little story telling of when we were expecting our daughter and had gone to an old auction house to see if we could find an antique rocking chair for her room.

All the while we were telling the story, our friend Bryan was rocking away in that very chair.

We told of how it was only our first time at bidding on an auction, and that we really weren't too sure of how the process worked.

This beautiful old rocking chair filled with lots of character and charm came up on the auction block. I kept on poking Jude in his side and giving him *that look*, but he just kept hesitating to give the auctioneer any kind of sign that he wanted to bid on the chair.

"*SOLD*", the auctioneer said, and then it was too late, someone else had bought the rocking chair.

Bryan got up to grab another beer from the fridge as we continued to tell the story…

After the auction ended, Jude found the guy that won the bid on the old rocking chair, offered him a quick little profit and we ended up getting that chair after all.

So, with a beer in his hand, Bryan walked back into the room, sat back down in the rocker, the seat broke into three separate pieces and the chair just collapsed right from under him.

Coincidence? Or not! You decide…Creepy old chair?

Creepy old chair.

Bedtime Stories

Plastic Wrap

Just when you think things can't get any more bizarre, then that one thing happens and you realize there is always something that can top it.

Sometimes people stop breathing repeatedly during their sleep, even hundreds of times. This is what happens to a person with untreated sleep apnea. It's a serious sleep disorder that occurs when breathing is interrupted. The brain as well as the rest of the body may not get enough oxygen, resulting in many health issues, including depression, which can also lead to suicide.

Twelve in one hundred thousand people die by suicide annually. It is viewed as a crime in some countries, and in most forms of Christianity, it's considered a sin.

Everything seems to be fine on the outside, but what's really going on inside? Comedians, hilariously funny guys like Robin Williams, and even a nephew of mine, and then there was Cyrus.

Cyrus, a single guy in his midforties, leased somewhat of an upscale property from me, seemed like a happy-go-lucky kind of guy, always cracking jokes. Some I understood, but if you know me, either it takes me forever to get it or I don't, but I'll laugh at your joke anyway.

Never suspecting that Cyrus was having a difficult time, I got a call from his boss. A bit strange, I thought, but I guessed since Cyrus had no family around, his boss thought that he should make me aware of a recent incident that involved one of his employees.

Some of Cyrus's work buddies just happened to stop by his house on their lunch hour to see why he hadn't shown up for work that day. When no one answered the door, while walking back to their truck, one of the guys happened to hear a car running in the garage. After banging on the garage door with no response, one of the guys broke a bedroom window to get inside of the house. Cyrus pulled through but quickly brushed the incident off as having fallen asleep in his car with it running, but his boss was suspicious and concerned enough to call me.

A few months passed and it was now football season. On their way to a game, his buddies from work came by to pick Cyrus up. Again, no one answered the door, but through the front door window, they could see Cyrus lying on the sofa in the living room. They rang the bell and banged on the door, but he didn't move a muscle. Frantic, one of the guys broke the window, reached in, and unlocked the door. Unfortunately, it was just too late. Cyrus had succeeded this time, having wrapped his own head tightly with plastic wrap, and had suffocated himself.

Next thing I knew, I was dealing with family members, lawyers, and landlords.

Cyrus's sister, who had been living out of state, called to break the awful news to me. She explained that Cyrus had a hard time in dealing with his sleep apnea and had always been depressed. I remember telling her how surprised I was and that he had always seemed like a happy-go-lucky kind of guy.

I found myself stuck in the middle between the family and lawyers wanting to have an estate sale on the property, which the owner did not want. The owner wanted to charge Cyrus's estate for things that were clearly not Cyrus's fault, such as rekeying locks, cleaning old draperies that hadn't been cleaned in years, the leaking dishwasher. Worst of all, nearly $6,000 "for Cyrus *intentionally* breaking his lease."

Now here's a secondhand story as told to me by a colleague of mine. So he walked up to the front door of a home that was scheduled to be sold at a foreclosure sale. The big note taped to the front door said "Fuck you!" He thought twice about it and decided, "Yeah, I don't think I want any part of this one." Later he's talking to a fellow foreclosure sale goer who had a horrifying tale to tell.

After winning the bid on that very same property and accompanied by his locksmith, the investor walked up to the front door. Just as my colleague did, he found a note taped to the front door. Only this time, it read something like this: "If you're reading this, I am already dead. Contact my son, his number is XXX-XXX-XXXX." So the locksmith drilled out the lock, he opened the front door, and *bang*—they heard a gun go off inside!

RIP to all those who felt their lives were so broken, they felt the need to take God's work into the hands of their own.

Something to think about.

Suicide is a purely selfish act. Consider all the people in one's life that will be left behind and broken. Remember, the present situation should not be the final destination. Please, just ask someone for help.

Dedicated to Justin.

May 01, 1993 – August 27, 2014

Happy Holidays

B*ang, bang, bang* on the front door of seventy-five-year-old Margaret Rader at 2:00 a.m. on a cold Monday morning. Being an "early to bed, early to rise" type of gal, she was not awakened out of bed but was shaken a bit by the sudden pounding on her door in the still of the night.

"POLICE!" Margaret heard the officers booming voice shout.

"What in the world," she thought.

Margaret opened the door. Instantly, the officer began to apologize profusely for waking her in the middle of the night. "But, ma'am, dispatch received a concern of thick slush and ice building up on the street right in front of your rental house in O'Fallon."

"Oh dear. There must be a broken pipe in the yard," Margaret said.

"No, ma'am, the water is coming from a broken pipe on the second story of the house," the officer explained. "All the utilities have been cut off and the house has been secured."

Well, of course, it was the middle of the night and way too cold for an elderly lady to go out in the middle of the night, and besides, the street and yard was a sheet of ice from water pouring out of the house for only God knows how long!

So who you gonna call when things go wrong? Bright and early on Monday morning, Margaret was calling and I just couldn't believe what she was telling me.

"Where in the hell are the tenants and why was the heat off?" Margaret said softly.

See, you had to know Margaret. I had managed her rental properties for years. She wasn't mad. She always just had a bit of sarcasm about her. She cussed a lot and would always tell me that she just wished the good Lord would take her but in a sarcastic sort of way.

"I'm not sure why the heat is off, but the tenants are out of town for the holidays. They called just before Christmas to let us know they would be in Florida visiting relatives until after New Year's."

"Oh no," Margaret said. "What a thing to come home to."

"I can't imagine, but let me give you a call back after I take a look."

Street crews had worked to clear the street, but there were still a few inches of slush at the curb. The driveway, sidewalk, and front porch were a sheet of ice. Water-soaked drywall littered the yard. Icicles were hanging from the second story and streams of ice covered the siding, windows, and shutters. CAUTION tape was draped across the front of the house. Orange stickers and yellow papers hung from the living room windows. The house was condemned!

"Oh boy, this isn't going to be good," I mumbled to myself under my breath.

I maneuvered my way across the frozen grass to the front of the house and opened the door. With wide eyes, my jaw dropped and I was in awe. I had never seen anything quite like this. The floor was covered in pink cotton-candy-looking stuff! Yes, and all the tenants' furniture was covered in pink insulation, and their Christmas tree and half of the drywall had just fallen right off the ceiling, saturated with water from the broken pipes. I walked over to the digital thermostat on the living room wall and the low battery symbol on the display was flashing on and off. The batteries had gone dead, and so the thermostat had quit working!

Back at the office, I called Margaret and her insurance company, and I called the tenants, who were on their way home from their Florida Christmas vacation. Surprisingly enough, they actually took the news quite well and even cracked a few jokes like, "Oh well, we were gonna take down the Christmas tree anyway when we got home. Ha-ha."

Happy holidays.

Streams of ice covered the siding windows and shutters.

The floor was covered in pink cotton-candy-looking stuff.

Let Sleeping Dogs Lie

During the mortgage meltdown in 2009, you could pick up some pretty good deals on real estate. Just about anywhere you looked.

But Vin and his wife, were looking for love in all the wrong places.

They just couldn't pass up the seemingly great deal on a small two-bedroom bungalow they had just fallen in love with.

And so, they purchased the inexpensive little house.

It wasn't in the best location, and you know what they say about real estate—location, location, location!

I had been the property manager of several rental properties for Vin and his wife over the years, but this one was not in my marketing area.

They were on their own this time. It was one house that I refused to manage and for good reason!

Oh, believe me. When Vin first began to talk to me about buying foreclosed properties in that area, I was upfront with him.

I bluntly told him that I would not be interested in managing rental property outside of my area.

Quite frankly, I told him that he was nuts! And you can't be anymore upfront than that. Can you?

Just to give you some idea as to what they were up against . . .

All the copper pipe was stripped from the bungalow before the couple even closed escrow!

The air conditioner was stolen and some of the windows got broken, just the week after closing!

Vin was a sweet older man with a strong Carolina accent.

He and his wife were the nicest people you could ever want to meet. In fact, you could say that they were pushovers. They were willing to do anything for their tenants. All a person had to do was ask.

"Say, Vin, I think the deck needs to be stained," said Bob, a tenant living in one of the other homes that I managed for him. Or "The lawn needs to be fertilized." "I'd like a garage door opener." "Can you repaint this room for us?"

It was like, "Ask and ye shall receive!"

Whatever their tenants asked for, they got it.

As a rule, they always liked tinkering around and worked on the rental properties themselves.

This property was no exception to the rule.

From time to time Vin would stop by my office just to chitchat, and he would usually have an "off the wall" story to share with me.

One afternoon, after finishing up a small repair job at one of his rental houses, Vin dropped in on me.

"Hey, you're never gonna believe this," he said with a smile as he leaned up against the jam of the doorway to my office.

With his eastern accent, he had habit of beginning most of his sentences with "Hey."

"Our tenant over in the other county called me. She was having a problem with one of the electrical outlets in one of the bedrooms. So I scheduled an appointment with her this morning. She said that her boyfriend would be there because he's not working right now. I got there around ten or so this morning but I couldn't get anyone to come to the door."

Vin continued. "I rang the doorbell and knocked, but no one came to the door. I called the gal on her cell phone. So she said that she'd call her boyfriend and wake him up. I was waiting on the front porch when all of a sudden, the front door swung open. But the guy didn't invite me in. I caught a glimpse of someone in the hallway disappearing around the corner," Vin explained.

Vin took a step inside the doorway and yelled, "Hello?" But no one answered him.

Vin crept into the hallway and said, "Which outlet isn't working?" Again, no one answered.

He walked down the hallway, peeking into the first tiny bedroom, but it was empty.

When he got to the last bedroom, he was surprised to see that someone was in the bed.

The person who had finally came to the door to let him in the house was in the bed!

He was going back to sleep!

Vin cleared his throat and raised his voice. "Hello . . . uh, sir?"

"Yeah," the man under the covers grumbled.

"Hey, I'm here to fix the outlet that's not working. Which one is it?" Vin asked.

Without uttering a sound, the man poked his hand out from under the covers and pointed to the outlet on the wall beside his bed.

"You've got to be kidding me," Vin thought. "This guy's just gonna stay in bed? He expects me to work right next to the bed? With him in it? Well, I've driven all the way here, so I may as well take a look at the outlet."

Vin took a screwdriver out of his tool bag and removed the outlet cover.

He was assessing the situation when . . . *Zzzzzzz.*

The guy began to snore!

"I couldn't believe my ears!" said Vin.

"No way! You have got to be kidding me!" I said. "The guy just stayed in bed, and while you were working right next to him?"

"Oh, just wait." he laughed. "It gets even better!"

"I determined that it wasn't the wall outlet after all. But the light switch that controlled the particular outlet was not working."

So he ran to the local hardware store to buy a new light switch and grab a quick bite to eat for lunch.

But when he returned, he walked up to the door and tried to turn the knob.

The door was locked again!

Now, he was losing his patience. Vin pounded on the door. "I need to get back in to fix the light switch!" he shouted.

But no one came to the door.

"Brother, I can't believe this guy. It's afternoon!" Vin thought. "I guess I'll have to call this gal again so she can call her lazy boyfriend to get him back out of bed to let me in again!"

As he began to dial the phone, he quickly hung it back up. He thought, "I'll just go around to the back of the house and knock on the bedroom window. Maybe he'll hear me knocking on the window and come unlock the door."

So Vin walked around to the backyard and opened the gate to the fence.

He could see a dog sleeping in its doghouse, and he just assumed that it was chained up.

Well, he assumed wrong!

Because as soon as he closed the gate and took a few steps into the backyard—*charge*! A white pit bull dog came racing toward him; it was snarling and barking at him!

"That dog was vicious! Why, he would have ripped my leg off!" exclaimed Vin.

He wheeled around and ran as fast as he could, but there was no time to open the gate.

He jumped over the fence, but not before the dog snapped at his leg and tore his blue jeans.

Vin sat down on the bumper of his older-model light-blue minivan to catch his breath and count his blessings.

"I am not having a good day! I just came within an inch of my life," he said to himself.

"Is this place really worth it?" he thought.

After catching his breath, he dialed his tenant's number.

"Hello? Hey, your dog just tried to maul me to death! Hey, I had to go to the store to get a part, and when I got back to the house, the door was locked. So I was going to go knock on your boyfriend's window and got attacked by your dog! Hey, you're not supposed to have a dog—not a dog like that, anyway!"

"I'm sorry," she said, "I can't believe he's still in bed." She circumvented the whole dog issue.

"I can't either!" Vin said with a little hint of sarcasm.

"I'll call him and have him unlock the door right away."

Impatiently, Vin waited on the front porch as several moments passed by.

Just like before, the door swung open. Vin was only able to catch a glimpse of the man's shadow disappearing in the hallway.

This time, he already knew where the tenant's boyfriend would be.

You guessed it—he was already back in the bed.

And before Vin finished replacing the light switch, *zzzzzzz*, the guy was snoring again!

I told Vin, "There is absolutely, positively *no way* that I would have stayed there to finish the job! *Would you?*"

After the tenants vacated, over a half a dozen empty alcohol bottles were left in the corner of the bedroom.

All-Time Highs

Ah, the early 1980s.
America needed a change and Ronald Reagan had just been elected our fortieth president of the United States.

Well, if you happened to be in the real estate business or thought of buying or selling real estate, then you'll probably remember the historically high interest rates. Interest rates were at an all-time high, soaring to 18 percent for a mortgage loan, making it difficult for most to realize the American dream of homeownership. It seemed more like the all-American nightmare. Thank God, my husband, Jude, brought a steady paycheck home every week, or we would never have survived with two kids to support and another on the way.

Some say those were their best years. We used alternative methods to get the job done like owner financing, contract for deed, and something called pledge shares, which I never understood.

The interest rate wasn't the only thing at an all-time high. The era was short-lived but long enough to force many real estate companies and mortgage companies alike to sell the business or close their doors. The company I worked for was no exception.

Afraid my past clients would lose track of me and having worked for a franchise company at that time in my career, I thought it was important to keep my name associated with the franchise as I bounced from one real estate office to the next. Besides, all my clothes had the franchise name embroidered on them. Funny how a silly little thing like that will influence your decision-making process when you're young and naive.

And so when the franchise office that I worked for was purchased by an unscrupulous broker from outside the area who didn't like to pay his agents or employees, I took my listings and bounced from office to office. Finally I landed at an independent company I've called home for the past thirty-five years.

But it was sure a long bumpy road getting there! First, I placed my real estate license at a small franchise office just a few miles from my old office, not realizing just how small it was until my first day answering the phones. Except the phones weren't ringing. So I decided to get acquainted with all the other listings in my new office. Much to my surprise, six of the ten or so listings that the company had happened to be mine!

"Boy, was I ever in the wrong place," I thought.

But I stuck it out until my listings either expired or were taken off the market because they just weren't selling.

Next stop, another franchise office just a few blocks further on down the road. By now I had learned to ask a few more questions about the company, like "How many listings does your office have?"

I was so excited. It was my first day with the new company, and it was also caravan day. A chance to meet everyone in my new office! We had one new listing to tour, so after a short office meeting all the agents climbed into one of the guys old ten-passenger window vans. Remember those? As we drove along, you could hear a pin drop. Nobody was saying a word. I couldn't help but notice that everyone in the van was at least forty to sixty years older than I was (I was in my midtwenties). I kept trying to strike up a conversation, but no one would talk to me about anything, not even the weather. I felt awkward and could not help but wonder if I hadn't made yet another mistake.

We pulled up in front of the small house and everyone quietly exited the van without uttering a word. The older gray-haired man that had driven the old window van rang the doorbell, but no one came to answer the door. He put the key into the lock, opened the door a crack, and shouted, "Hello?"

He swung the door open and everyone began to go inside. I heard one of the ladies say, "Well, aren't you a pretty thing."

Standing there on the little concrete front porch, I could hear a lot of chatter and laughter going on inside. I walked into the house and in the center of the living room stood a gorgeous white German shepherd just looking at all of us with her head cocked to one side and happily wagging her tail.

"Well, hello there, girl," one of the guys said in his booming voice.

"Oh, what a beautiful dog," another woman said.

Everyone was petting the dog and talking about how well behaved she was. Prancing around the room, every now and then she would whimper or bark softly. We were all playing with the dog, laughing and talking to one another. For the first time all morning, someone had finally spoken to me!

Then just like always on house tour, everyone began to scatter about the house. I was looking at the kitchen, when suddenly two of the ladies came running into the room. They were flailing their arms all around, hopping up and down, bumping into each other, and pointing down the hallway to the bedrooms. They were both trying to tell me something but neither of them could utter a sound.

"What's wrong?" I asked.

But they were simply speechless. Then another lady ran into the kitchen and without saying a word, grabbed hold of my sweater, and pulled me through the living room and out onto the front porch.

Once again, I asked, "What is going on?"

In the front yard, all three women were trying to say something to me but weren't making a sound. They looked like a little trio of mimes! Just then, a couple of the men came walking out the front door and were laughing out loud. One of the three women finally blurted out, "THERE'S A NAKED MAN IN THE BEDROOM!"

"Oh, you're kidding me, how'd I miss that!" I said.

One of the men laughed and said, "Yeah, he's lying flat on his back and not a stitch of clothes on."

Another said, "No covers on either."

One of the other guys said, "He might be asleep but *it's* sure not."

The guys all laughed.

"Are you sure he's really sleeping?" I asked.

"Well, he's sure snorin' away."

I chuckled along with the men and the women just looked at me.

With that, we all piled into the van to head back to the office. Instantly the chatter stopped and again; no one said a word. Riding along, I thought to myself, what had just happened was absolutely hilarious yet nobody was saying a word. We should still be laughing and cracking jokes all the way back to the office! Like interest rates aren't the only thing that's high, if you know what I mean, ha-ha.

We had made enough noise to wake the dead when we were all petting and playing with the white German shepherd that had greeted us that morning, yet the homeowner never even knew we were in his house, much less in his bedroom.

Once again, I tried to strike up a conversation about what had just happened back at the house, but no one wanted to talk about it.

I was right. I had made another mistake.

As soon as we arrived back at the office from house tour, I told the manager that I didn't belong there and would be leaving. He said that he understood and explained to me that he didn't think that I would last, not with the high interest rates.

High interest rates?

High interest rates didn't have a thing to do with my leaving his company after only one day on the job. It wasn't about the all-time highs but more like the all-time lows.

If you can't have a good laugh and conversation over something as bizarre as being in an unsuspecting naked homeowner's house, then what can you laugh and talk about?

Blackout

So what's the first thing you do when you get to your hotel room or vacation spot? You kick your shoes off and unpack, of course.

Jude and I had just gotten to our little place at the lake, always arriving late at night after getting home from work on a Friday evening.

Our ritual—Jude heads to the dock to dump the minnows in the floating minnow bucket that my sister, Karen, had bought for us, and he's not kidding anyone. I'm sure he throws a cast or two before coming back up to unpack the cooler. I get busy putting the groceries away and all the new stuff we'd (I'd) bought for the place, that the bed of our truck is always filled with every time we come.

After settling down on the sofa and crossing my legs to relax a little, Jude said, "What is on the bottom of your socks?" I looked at the bottom of my white socks and they were pitch-black! "What in the?" I thought. We started looking around at the place and began to find a black smeary substance on *everything*. After a little closer look, and we found that there's a large jar with black soot coating the inside of it. One on the bar and another in the bedroom. Large jar candles, a little strange because we don't have any candles at the lake.

We didn't want our guests playing with fire. See, our condo has always been on a nightly rental program where we offer it to vacationers to rent out for a weekend or even a week or two.

Evidently, our last guest stopped at the store on the way to our place and bought the largest scented jar candles they could find. The candles had to have burned the entire weekend because the wicks had been burned right down to the bottom of the jar.

Black soot from the untrimmed wicks of the candles covered everything. Cabinets, light fixtures, and even the toilet and the furnace filter were black with soot. Ugh. How could housekeeping have missed all of this?

Next morning, I asked our neighbor Linda if she had noticed anything over the weekend. She laughed. "Wayne and I noticed their car didn't move all weekend. It was bright orange with huge chrome wheels, so we would have noticed if they had gone anywhere. Another thing we noticed was on Sunday, the patio door was open all morning and the front door was propped open. We thought it was funny because you don't have a screen door, plus we could hear that the air conditioning was running with the doors and windows open." I kept sneaking around and peeking out of the windows just trying to find out what they were up to!

"Yeah." I scowled. "They were airing all the smoke out of the place!" Then I told Linda about the jar candles and soot everywhere.

I could just imagine what they were doing in my condo all weekend, if you know what I mean. But when I called my property manager Rusty to complain that we were not informed of the damage, he didn't have a clue because the housekeeper had not reported it. He also had different ideas about what went on there.

"I think they were probably cooking meth. Do you mind if I show your furnace filter to the police and have it tested?" Rusty asked.

"Are you nuts? You've got to be kidding me, no way! I will not have the law come in and tear my place apart searching for something that's really nothing. I told you. The people you rented my condo to burned candles all weekend long. The candles were left in the condo and were burned all the way to the bottom of the jars, and the inside of the jars are black. There's no chemical smell in here, just a black smeary residue all over everything."

I told Rusty that I wanted everything professionally cleaned from top to bottom—walls, ceilings, carpet, furniture, lamps, everything, and please not by his housekeeping staff.

Years after the candle incident, we still find a little soot here and there.

The Nature of the Beast

Cops Buy Houses Too

They really do! As one not so smart teenager learned the hard way.

My longtime client Edward was a city cop. He had sort of a northeastern accent and he's always reminded me of Danny DeVito, who played Louie De Palma in the popular late '70s, early '80s sitcom *Taxi*. Although Edward was quite a bit taller and better looking than DeVito (sorry, Danny).

Anyway, Edward was ready to buy another investment property.

And so I set out to search for the proverbial good deal.

The house had to be a ranch-style home. Three bedrooms and preferably two full baths, a basement and either a carport or at least a one car garage. And it had to be a good deal and be able to turn a decent profit.

Those were Edward's only requirements.

"That shouldn't be too hard to come up with," I told Ed.

In fact, a little one-thousand-square-foot ranch-style home caught his eye on the very first day of our search for the perfect house. It was around twenty years old and pretty beat up but it had a bonus—a two-car garage and it had already been leased.

We had just finished looking at the basement and kitchen, then on to check out the bedrooms we went.

We were standing there in the master bedroom discussing the house and all its great potential. All of a sudden without any warning, from underneath the king-size bed, a tiny little dog came charging at me.

The little dog with shimmery copper-and-gray fur repeatedly kept attacking my ankles!

It was happening so fast that neither of us knew just quite what to do.

Edward yelled for the teenager that had been lounging in the living room watching TV.

"HEY, KID! COME GET YOUR DOG!"

But he didn't come to my rescue.

I just kept hopping around the room in my short skirt and high heels with my notebook in one hand and my purse dangling off my shoulder.

The little dog just kept barking at me and biting my ankles.

Finally, Edward scooped it up, threw it in the closet, and slammed the door shut.

The little dog was so tiny. Even though it must have bitten me nine or ten times on my ankles, it's tiny little teeth never once broke the skin.

"You okay?" my buyer asked.

"I'm just a little shaken up but I'm fine."

Then we both just looked at each other and broke into laughter.

Why me? The little dog had targeted me and only me! Edward didn't have a dog, and neither did I. The only thing that I could think of was that maybe the ferocious little dog had smelled Muffy, a smelly, scruffy old dog that Karie would sneak inside my house and hide. I might hear something inside the closet in her room and open the door, and there would be Muffy just sitting there in the dark.

Maybe the dog had smelled her scent on me, or maybe it didn't like high heels, or maybe it just didn't like women in general.

As we were leaving the house, we passed through the living room where the teenager was still lying on the sofa.

He was glued to the TV and totally oblivious to what had just happened to us.

As we were walking out the front door, Edward said, "Hey, your dog just bit her. You really should put it away whenever somebody comes to look at the house. It's not a very good selling point, ya know? By the way, your dog's in the closet." Edward told the boy.

I knew my client liked the house, and I thought it would be a good investment for him too. So as we were both getting into our cars, I said, "Well, think it over and just give me a call if you'd like to make an offer."

"Yeah sure, I'll let ya know if I decide to make, um, an offer. You sure you're okay?" Edward asked.

"Yes, I'm fine. Don't worry about me."

On the way home, I picked up my daughter, Karie, from my mom's house.

I wasn't home fifteen minutes and the phone rang.

It was Edward.

"Hey, if it's okay, I'd like to take a second look at that house on my way to work this afternoon."

"That's fine, but I've already changed clothes and I'll have to bring my little girl with us. I've just picked her up from the babysitters."

"No problem," he said. "Okay, meet you there in thirty?"

"We'll be there."

So with my four-year-old daughter in tow. I met Edward back at the house for a second look.

With Karie in my arms, I rang the doorbell but no one came to the door.

Then I rang the bell again.

The door finally opened. The tall thin teenager with dark shoulder-length hair leaned up against the door jam and just stood there looking at us.

"Hi," I said. "I'm Nancy, I'm here to show the house again."

"Yeah? So why the cop?" the teenage boy asked.

"What?" I asked.

Confused, Edward and I both just looked at each other.

I looked back at the teenager and said, "We're just here to see the house again. We were here earlier, remember?"

"Then why'd you bring a cop?" the teenage boy asked with a lot of attitude.

The boy had obviously thought I had called the police about the episode with his dog that happened just a few hours earlier in the day.

Edward, or Officer Edward Sutter, I should say, was just on the way to his second shift job and was dressed in his uniform.

From his official police officers hat and uniform with a shiny badge pinned to his chest, holster complete with gun and all, right down to his black spit shined shoes.

The boy didn't recognize Edward in his police uniform as the man that had looked at the house earlier in the day. I was wearing my blue jeans and had my daughter in my arms. He just thought that I had called the police about his dog biting me and was sure that was why we were there.

Officer Sutter looked at the boy and said, "Cops buy houses too, ya know."

Well, Edward did buy the house after all, in spite of its little extra selling feature.

The boy and his family remained in the home and the tiny little ferocious dog too.

This story appeared in the national publication of REALTOR®, "in the trenches."

The Monster Buck

It was the last Sunday in October, and it had been an absolutely beautiful day. Jude and I had just arrived home that evening after a long drive from our weekend place at the lake.

We could hear the phone ringing as we walked in the door. I hesitated to answer and then just decided to let the machine get it. The last thing I wanted to do that Sunday evening after driving for three hours was to get caught up on the phone call. Monday morning would come soon enough, I thought to myself.

We finished unpacking our bags and unloading our catch from the weekend from the cooler and into the fridge, but before retiring for the night, I decided to listen to my messages.

It was from one of my landlords that lived in the land of ten thousand lakes who just also happened to be my best friend, Mary Jo. She and her husband, Rod, had moved there two years ago. They had left their home in my care to locate a tenant and manage as a rental property. Rod had taken a job with the airlines and was working in Minneapolis.

I pressed Play on the machine.

"Nancy, please call me. I need to talk to you about our tenants."

Usually Jo was very bubbly and happy, but she sounded serious.

It was getting late, but I knew if I waited until morning to return her call, I would be awake most of the night wondering what she wanted, so I went ahead and called her right back.

She answered the phone on the first ring.

"Hi there!"

"Listen, Nancy, Rachel called today and she was so upset." Rachel, Rod and Jo's daughter, was still attending college here in Missouri.

Erin, a neighborhood friend of Rachel's, was taking a walk, and when she walked past our old house, she was shocked at what she thought she had seen in the walnut tree in the backyard, Jo said.

"Nancy, Erin thinks that she saw a deer stand in the tree."

"No way," I shouted. "Your tenants love the deer as much as you guys did when you lived there. Remember last summer? They came into my office to pay the rent and told me that they had bought an automatic feeder for the deer and turkey."

Their house was a modest white two-story and was very well kept and located in a well-established suburban neighborhood. The backyard bordered a beautiful creek with thick woods and an abundance of wildlife. Earlier in the spring, I had rented the house to Mike and Robbie, a young couple from Indiana.

I had told them all about the animals that lived in the woods and how they would come to the yard to feed almost every day. Rod and Jo loved the deer and had been feeding them corn for the past several years just on the other side of the creek. They had even spotted a twelve-point buck just before moving to Minnesota.

The tenants were ecstatic about all the wildlife that lived in the woods behind their new Missouri home.

"It's like *Wild Kingdom* at night," Mike said with excitement as he handed his rent over to me. "Yeah, we even went out and bought an automatic feeder. We feed the deer, raccoons, and turkeys. I even feed the fish in the creek."

"Wow, you must really enjoy it. I'm happy that you like it there."

"Yeah, Robbie and I can't wait for it to get dark. We go outside and just wait for the show to begin."

That Sunday evening, Jo and I both felt the same way. Erin most likely had seen something else and mistakenly just thought it was a deer stand.

"That's just got to be it," I told Mary Jo. "Mike and Robbie seem to love the deer as much as you and Rod. I promise to take a drive by the house this week and check it out."

Little did I know that it would be too late.

In an unseasonably warm early November morning, I decided to go by my friend's house on Wednesday before driving to the office. It was around 8:45 a.m. as I rolled to a stop in front of the sparkling clean white two-story. I could already see the deer stand up in the walnut tree that stood on the edge of the creek in the backyard. There was no mistake about it. It definitely had the makings of a deer stand with its wooden steps nailed to the trunk of the tree and about ten feet in the air, a small platform just big enough for a hunter to sit.

It was obvious the deer stand was facing in the same direction of where I knew the deer had always been fed. Rod and Jo had always fed them on the other side of the creek away from the house.

My heart just sank.

Staring at the tree, from the corner of my eye, I saw something moving on the opposite bank of the creek. A man dressed in a camo colored jacket and baseball cap was talking on his cell phone and waving a compound bow around as if he were using it to make gestures as he spoke. Then a young woman with long dark blond hair, also dressed in a camo colored sweatshirt, came climbing up from inside of the creek. It was a deep wet weather creek with steep banks that had been shored up with large rocks to keep the banks from eroding. She immediately walked to the rear corner of the house, tilted her head, and looked at me with a puzzled look on her face. We stared at each other for a moment, and then she quickly disappeared behind the house. When I turned my attention back to the man on the other side of the creek, he had vanished. I kept on looking for him. But where could he have gone? Just then, I saw a tiny bit of movement coming from behind a tree. Was he was hiding from me? I couldn't believe it—he was actually hiding from me. I just sat there in my car. I wasn't sure what to do, and I certainly didn't know what they were doing. Next, I saw the bow that the man had in his hand when he was talking on his cell phone fly across the creek toward the house, but I couldn't see where it had landed. I was really puzzled now. Why would he just toss an expensive piece of hunting equipment onto the ground? A moment later, several sticks came flying over the creek. By now, I was just dumbfounded. What in the world were these two doing?

I decided to drive down the block to phone my manager. Douglas was at a Veterans Day breakfast meeting when he answered the phone. He could see from the caller ID that it was a call from one of his rental managers.

"Adult day care," he answered.

I just laughed at him because that was how he often answered the phone when he knew that one of his rental managers were calling. I began to explain to him that Erin's story about the deer stand in the tree was true and told him all about how the tenants had been in the backyard acting so strange. He began to laugh. "Boy, you really come up with some crap, don't you?" He chuckled. Douglas suggested that I just go to the door and explain to them that they need to remove the deer stand and that a neighbor had complained and there was no hunting allowed on the property.

Mike must have seen me pull onto the driveway or may have heard my car door shut. I was walking up to the front door when he came racing from around the side of the garage to the front of the house.

"Hi, how are ya? Why are you here?" he asked as he gasped for breath.

"I'm here because I received a complaint about your deer stand."

Gasping for breath and sweating profusely, Mike replied, "It's only for practice. I was practicing because I'm going hunting this afternoon."

As I laughed under my breath, I thought to myself, "He's out of breath. Is he practicing chasing the deer?"

Just then, Mike bent over and clutched his knees. He was hyperventilating.

With concern, I asked. "You okay?"

"Yeah, I'm just out of breath from practicing." He could barely speak.

I laughed again and thought, "Yeah, he must be practicing chasing those damn deer." But as Mike was bending over holding his knees, I noticed that his blue jeans were wet up to the knees and there was blood on his pants leg.

It reminded me of a little wardrobe malfunction that I had when I saw Mike clutch his knees. Once during an annual inspection of the house, we were just about finished when I felt one of my thigh's high hose beginning to slip. With every step, I could feel it sliding a little lower, but Mike and Robbie were walking behind me, so I couldn't pull it up. I almost made it out of the front door, and then my hose just fell down. They just kept talking to me and I couldn't get away, so I just stood there on the front porch, listening to them chatter. Chatter was all I heard because all I could think of was the hosiery around my ankle! When I finally made my getaway, I had to pull over because I was laughing so hard at myself.

Anyhow . . .

Mike was a tall nice-looking young man with sandy-colored hair. Whenever he had come into my office to pay the rent, he was always well groomed and dressed very nice. He seemed to be a well-mannered businessman and was always very calm and collected. I had never seen him look or act like this before. It quickly became clear to me that I must be in the right place at the right time and that Mike was surely in the wrong place at the wrong time. I had him cornered and I knew it. I began to feel very uncomfortable in the compromising situation that I realized that I had found myself in.

Still bent over and clutching his knees, suddenly Mike caught his breath and looked up at me. "Who complained?" he asked.

"A neighbor," I replied.

Then he began to ramble from one thing to the next. "I just can't believe anyone would complain about us. We get along with the neighbors. We take great care of the yard. I didn't realize we were causing any problems. I even saved an abandoned kitten in the pouring rain from the vacant lot next door, and we took it to a no-kill shelter. I've bow-hunted in the woods, a guy in the court bow-hunts back there too, and so does Denny, just down the street."

What? An abandoned kitten? Neighbors hunting? I thought, "Where is all of this coming from, or better yet, where is it going?"

I became even more uncomfortable with the way Mike was behaving and decided that it was time for me to go. It was obvious that he was extremely nervous and upset about something, and whatever it was, I was sure it was lying dead right out there in backyard.

"Just take the deer stand down," I said. "It's upsetting the neighbors, and the owners of the house do not want any hunting on the property. They like the deer and so do a lot of the neighbors."

"If that stand is bothering the neighbors, I'll take it down," Mike quickly agreed. "I just use it for target practice. I'm on vacation this week and I'm just going hunting for a few days. Next week, you won't see me like this. I'll get cleaned up and be back at my job."

I was never so happy to be on my way to the office and out of the situation I had found myself in. Driving to the office, I recounted the morning's events. The thing that still seemed odd to me was why he tossed his bow and a bunch of sticks over the creek and into the yard. Then it hit me—"Of course, the arrows." What I thought looked like a few sticks flying through the air were actually his arrows. He must have shot a deer with his bow in the backyard and was worried that I was going to get out of my car, walk into the backyard, and discover what he had done. Then I recalled how Robbie had disappeared behind the house. She must have picked up the bow, gathered up the arrows, and put them in the nearby storage shed that Rod had built for his lawn tractor. Finally, at my office I settled in as I usually do. I set up my laptop, read a few messages that were on my desk, checked my email, and began listening to my voice mail. There were a few messages from the night before as well as that morning, but there was one that was particularly interesting to say the least. It was a long, babbling message from Mike.

"You caught me off guard this morning. Uh, the first thing I want to let you know is, I do not hunt in these woods for deer. The only thing that's back here are little baby does and I feed them, and uh, and I, I do exactly as I told you I do. I feed all these animals back here. You can ask Denny next door to me. He knows that I don't shoot these deer. He knows the deer that I have on my wall. Uh, I am a big deer hunter. I just so happened to be out at my brother's house this morning in a town about an hour and a half from here and I shot a monster buck, and I was in the process of cleaning him. So I would have been guilty by association. You caught me in a bad situation. That tree stand in my yard is simply for practice. I am an avid bow hunter and I take a lot of pride in my ability to hunt. They are just too small, these suburban deer. But I would never shoot these deer, and I want you to call me back. I just, well, you caught me off guard. If I would have taken you around back, you would have said there is no way that big buck was in these woods. But uh, anyway, I have several places to hunt, on real farms. I would not hunt in my backyard. Please call me, I want to talk to you about this. Yeah, that's why I was breathing hard. You caught me in a bad situation. That stand is coming down. I will never have that stand in my backyard again. I did not know I was causing problems with the neighbors. Please call me back, I want to talk to you about this."

After listening to his message and several hours later, I still didn't know what to do about the situation. I talked with others in my office who offered their advice, but there were some who were not very sensitive to my dilemma, like Jerry, who was one of my comedian coworkers. While I was on an important phone call, there was Jerry outside my office window, pretending to pull back on the string of a compound "air" bow to shoot a pretend deer. That was just the first of many deer jokes around the office to come, like when Ken announced at the weekly sales meeting that he would be out of town for several days deer hunting, and Jerry said, "If you don't get a deer, Nancy's got a good place for you to go hunting." Everyone laughed. And that year, at the office Christmas party, I was anonymously presented with a bobble-head buck dashboard statue. I never did find out who gave me the bobble-head deer, but I still have it on my desk at the office. The jokes just kept on coming for months. "Hey, Nancy, I set up a wildlife camera in my backyard and got a shot of a big old buck last night. I think I'll just set up a deer stand too," Ken joked. "Ha. Ha. Ha."

Anyway, I called the Department of Conservation, but their office was closed in observance of Veterans Day so I contacted the county sheriff just to ask general questions about hunting.

Finally, I just decided to call my friends to ask how they wanted me to handle the situation. After all, they were their tenants.

First, I called their house. There was no answer. Next, I called Mary Jo's cell phone and got her voice mail, so I left her a message.

Then I called Rod's cell. Same thing, voice mail.

Just a few moments passed and it was Rod calling me back. After I explained everything to him, he just laughed in amazement. "You're kidding me."

"No kidding."

"Why would he think that he could hunt in a subdivision like that?"

"You got me, I can't believe it either."

After some discussion, we agreed that what I had already told Mike earlier that day was probably enough. He should remove the deer stand and that he could not hunt or field dress animals on the property. Mike was scared that was pretty obvious. He was a decent guy that had just done something stupid. He'd been through a lot that day, and most likely wouldn't want to put himself through another day like today again, we thought. Rod suggested that I should write him a letter just to be on the safe side.

Before ending the conversation, I asked, "Are we going to tell Jo about this?"

Rod chuckled. "Yeah. I'll tell her. She'll probably get her feathers ruffled, but she'll get over it."

A short while after, I had hung up the phone from talking to Rod, then Jo called.

"Hi, have you talked to Rod yet?" I asked.

"No, why?" Jo sounded puzzled and concerned. It was unusual for me to call either one of them during the day. We both called each other several times a week but always in the evening because our days were so hectic.

I proceeded to explain what had happened that morning when I had gone to check out the deer stand. After listening to the story, Jo said, "Oh, I just feel like crying."

Rod and Jo knew the deer and their habits. After all, they had seen the same deer several times a week. They had even seen a nice buck a few times. "Oh, I'll bet he got my big buck." She was sick over it and so was I. To think that the deer had just came there to get something to eat and . . .

Well, it was nearly the end of the workday and time to return Mike's call. I was sure he must have been waiting in anticipation most of the day to hear back from me. "Hi, Mike, I'm returning your call."

"You got my message?"

I simply responded with, "Yes, and I don't believe you."

"I wish you would," Mike pleaded.

"Well, I don't believe that you killed a deer an hour and a half away, then drove it to your house and put it into the creek to clean it. That is something you do wherever you shoot the animal. There wasn't even a vehicle at your house this morning that could have even transported a deer."

The only cars at the house that morning were a nice midsize car on the driveway and the classic car in the garage that Mike had once told me that he had restored.

"My buddy had to get to work. He had to leave and he dropped me off this morning."

"There was no blood or fur on the driveway, and there were no drag marks or tire tracks in the yard this morning. I don't believe you, but this is what I want you to do. Take the stand down and do not hunt on that property or in the woods, and we'll leave it at that."

"The stand is gone, the steps are being taken down right now, and you will never see another piece of hunting equipment on the property," Mike promised.

You know what the experts always say—the number one rule in real estate is to put it in writing, and so I did.

> Dear Mike and Robbie:
>
> The owners of the property just wanted me to clarify that there is to be no hunting on the property or on the subdivision's common grounds, as you have stated that you as well as other neighbors have hunted there.

It is bow-hunting season. However, to hunt on the property or common grounds, you would need written permission to do so from the property owner or subdivision trustees. For this and other obvious reasons and not to mention the liability, permission would not be given. Furthermore, you may not discharge a weapon less than one hundred yards of a residential area, church, or school. There are a few suburban areas in our state that allow controlled hunting to "thin the herd"; however, this is not one of them.

With that having been said, regardless of where the deer was taken from on Wednesday, the owner requests that you not field dress animals on the property. He does not want to cause any of the neighbors to be upset.

Most of the neighbors enjoy the deer and, as you have said, may associate such a sight with being one of the local deer population. As long as everyone understands each other, there is no problem. The owners are happy that you enjoy the property and hope that you enjoy it enough to make it your home for a while.

If you have any questions or would like to further discuss the matter, feel free to call me anytime.

N. S. Jordan
Property Manager

A few days later, I drove past the house to make certain that the deer stand had been taken down. The stand was gone and all the wooden steps that had been nailed to the tree had been removed. But there was something that I had never noticed before about the house. Most of the leaves had fallen from the trees in the woods behind the house by now. I had always thought that the woods behind the house were pretty thick, but I could actually see the houses that bordered the woods in the neighboring subdivision. When I think of kids playing in backyards, it amazes me that anyone could possibly think that they could hunt in such a small patch of woods and surrounded by so many homes. So was the monster buck killed in the backyard or on the subdivision common grounds? Or on a farm an hour and a half away? We'll never know for certain, but I have a pretty good idea.

In fact, several months later when it was time to renew the lease, I received an email from Mike:

> Nancy, this is Mike, and I think we need to discuss leasing the house for one more year. I hope you have forgiven me for what happened last fall. Outside of that, I believe I have been a very good renter, and now that I know the rules, I will follow them.

PS, this is the story that inspired me to share my stories with you.

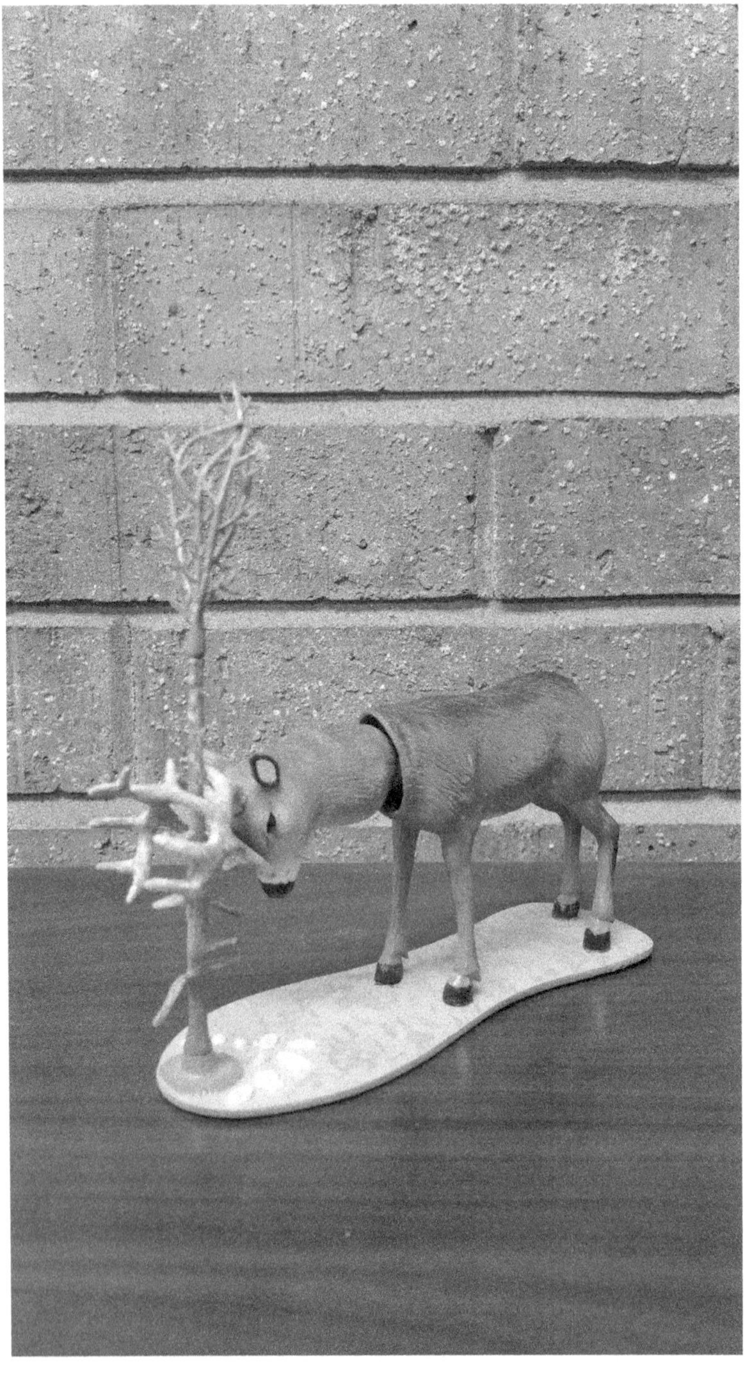

Oh, Do You Know the Muffin Man?

The note should have read "Friendly dog inside will bolt when door is opened, so get ready!"

Clients just couldn't wait to see the small house on Cherry Lane. We meet on the driveway quickly greeting one another in the misting rain, and on the front door of the house, there's a note.

The note read, "Friendly dog inside named Muffin."

Knock, knock. No one came to the door, so I took the key from the lock box and turned the lock on the door handle.

The very second I opened the door, this little white furry dog bolted right out the door.

"Oh my god!" I yelled, shoved the listing sheets into my client's hand, and chased after the dog.

I was running in the rain down Cherry Lane, trying to catch up with the white fur ball before it can get to the busy cross street, in black dress and heels, when I should be wearing track shoes, and my purse was dangling off my arm. I finally caught it when it decided to take a little break to water the Stop sign before running into the busy street.

Out of breath, I scooped it up and walked slowly back to the house, holding the dog closely to me so it couldn't escape again. My clients were laughing, my black dress was covered in white fur, and to top it off, I now smelled like a wet dog.

As if that's not bad enough, I met Robert in the hall back at the office, he asked, "Where've you been, get caught in the rain?"

"I've just been chasing a dog down the street in the rain. I've got dog fur all over me and I smell like a wet dog, that's all."

Bob leaned toward me, sniffed, laughed a little, and said, "You do smell" then skulked off.

♫ Oh, do you know the Muffin Man . . . ♪♪

Number 1 Breed

Jude and I, along with our two sons Jude Jr. and Jason (a do-it-yourself family), had worked all day at Jason's new rehab project, a large town house in the city.

As we dragged ourselves up the steps to our front door, we noticed something red smeared on the living room window glass and the white sheer curtains were spattered with bright red dots. Peering through the blood-smeared glass, it looked as if someone had been slaughtered right in our own living room! And through the narrow windows that flanked each side of the front door, we could see that blood smears covered the white ceramic-tiled floor in the foyer.

Jude hurried to unlock the door. Once inside, we were in awe of the blood-spattered walls and bloody smears all over our white leather furniture and carpeting. The room looked like a crime scene from Showtime's mystery series *Dexter*.

"Oh my god." The first thing that ran through my mind was Karie, our teenage daughter who had been home alone all day. "Karie!" I frantically screamed.

Our living room looked like the set of an Alfred Hitchcock movie. It was surreal!

Just as I was ready to lose my mind, our four-year-old yellow Labrador retriever mix named Maxwell appeared in the kitchen doorway. We called him Max for short and Uncle Max after our first grandkids were born. He was covered in blood from his front paws up to his shoulders.

I was relieved our daughter hadn't been harmed but was still concerned about our poor dog. After all, he was my little boy dressed up in a puppy suit, which was how I always referred to him.

Combing through his bloodstained fur, looking for some sort of terrible wound, I asked, "What in the world happened to you?" He started to pant and blood began to drip from his big pink tongue. "How'd you cut your tongue, boy?" I asked. Then I noticed the cabinet door under the kitchen sink standing open and the trash can had been dragged out onto the floor. Strewn about the room were empty cans, coffee grounds, and lots of trash. The dog must have cut his tongue on the jagged edge of a can, I thought. And trying to clean the blood from his paws, the more he licked, the more he became covered in it. The more blood-covered he became, the more nervous he got. And the more nervous he got, the more he panted and drooled until the house was covered in blood! Once I realized what had happened, my emotions went from pity for the poor animal to furious in sixty seconds. "MAXWELL, BAD DOG!" I yelled.

Our house was an absolute mess. There was blood and slobber from one end of the house to the other, on the floors, carpet, curtains, walls, and furniture. After painting and cleaning all day at Jason's condo, we were already pooped. And it took the four of us several more hours to clean up the bloody mess. It was by far a much bigger mess than the time the dog had gotten his collar hooked onto the bottom rack of the dishwasher.

Maxwell always loved to help clean up the kitchen after dinner. First, he would lick the crumbs off the floor. Then I would load the dishwasher with dirty dishes, and he would rinse them. With me saying "Max, no, get out, Maxwell, no" the whole time! Until one evening after dinner, "we" were busy rinsing and loading the dishwasher, and somehow, his choke chain collar got hooked on the bottom rack. Max tried to pull away and, with that, jerked the entire rack fully loaded with dirty dishes right out onto the kitchen floor. I'll never forget the sound of my dishes breaking into pieces. I immediately herded Max out of the room, fearing he would cut his paws on the broken glass that now covered my kitchen floor. Needless to say, Maxwell never helped with the dishes again.

A few weeks later, Jude and I had gone to our place at the lake for the weekend and had left Max at home with the kids. When we arrived home on Sunday evening, Max was acting peculiar, like he had done something wrong. We didn't think much of it and both raced for the bathrooms after the long drive.

"That's funny," I said. "There's no water in this toilet."

"There isn't any in this one either," Jude said.

It was getting late and we both needed to get up early for work the next morning. Before going to bed, I always closed the living room curtains, but when I stepped in front of the window, *squish*. I looked down and I was standing in a circle of pee two feet in diameter! When I looked at Maxwell, he just crouched down. But we didn't scold him. We knew something was wrong. He had drank both toilets and his water dish completely dry, he was panting uncontrollably and all he wanted was water, water, and more water. I know it's hard to believe, but he had never peed in the house, not even when he was just a little pup.

It took quite a while to remove the urine from the carpeting using nothing but a Shop-Vac. Then I noticed there was dog slobber all over the living room window too. Poor Maxwell must have waited and waited at that window for somebody, anybody to come home. It was almost as if he had given up hope and turned to walk away from the window, unable to take another step and then . . .

Even after all that, Maxwell was still the puppy love of my life, my little boy in a puppy suit. When he was just a cute little ten-week-old pup, we had "puppysat" for our oldest son, Jude Jr., who had gone hiking in the Colorado Mountains. But after two weeks, when Junior came to retrieve his puppy, I just couldn't part with him.

Five years after the Hitchcock incident, Maxwell developed diabetes, arthritis, and finally bone cancer. And so, after several months of insulin injections twice a day and variety of medications to make the dog comfortable, it was time to say goodbye.

The vet always said, "You'll know when the time comes." For Max, the time came on New Year's Day and we had to put our big yellow dog down.

On the way home from the emergency vet that day, we reminisced of Max standing in the bow of our boat flying down the lake at forty miles per hour with his ears flopping in the wind. When he got tired of standing, he would just back up and sit down with his paws on the floor and butt in the seat between us. He sat quietly with his doggy sunglasses ("doggles") on intently keeping watch on Jude's fishing pole. Max knew when he was about to set the hook, and just when the time was right, he'd jump up excited to watch him reel in the big fish. Like a Setter pointing out a Pheasant or something. The only thing Maxwell didn't enjoy about fishing was "big bird." That's what we always called the big blue heron that would fish in the pond behind our house. Max hated that bird, and whenever he would see a heron at the lake when we were fishing, he'd nearly come out of the boat after it. In fact, we often had to hold him back. We always joked that the dog must have thought that the big bird had followed him all the way from our house to the lake.

Earlier in the fall on my way to a listing appointment, I remembered driving past a small cemetery for pets. It was really just the low-lying portion of a cemetery that the water table was too high to bury humans. So they used the area to bury animals of all kinds. There was even a chimpanzee buried there. Four days after Maxwell was euthanized, I received a call from the cemetery asking us to come view his body before burying it.

"You're kidding, right?" I asked.

"No, ma'am, for legal reasons we ask for someone to view the body before burying it."

"But his eyes were open when he passed. I can't imagine after four days that he would still look good, and besides, that's not the way I want to remember him," I said. (If you're familiar with euthanasia, you'll know that sometimes an animal's eyes don't close when they pass.)

"Your dog looks very good, I can tell that he was loved."

"No, we don't want to see him," I insisted.

"Well then, you will need to be present when we seal the casket and lower it into the grave," the man said.

"How bizarre is this?" I thought.

I agreed that we would meet him at the little cemetery for pets after Jude and I got off work that day.

As we pulled into the entrance, Jude stopped the truck. We could see Maxwell's little gray casket made of heavy plastic sitting atop two-by-fours laid across the little grave. A bouquet of white lilies laid on top of it. Puzzled, we both just looked at one another.

I loved the dog but had never intended to attend a real funeral for him.

We gathered around—the grave digger with shovel in hand, the little man with thick glasses that I had spoken to on the phone, and Jude and me.

"Is there anything that you would like to say about your dog?" he asked.

"No, we're good," I said.

Then the little man and gravedigger bowed their heads and began to deliver Maxwell's eulogy.

With wide eyes, we both looked at each other and quickly bowed our heads. It was obvious these men took their job seriously and that was touching. I fought to hold back the tears but lost the battle.

We were so blindsided by the whole funeral thing for our dog that we had no idea what the man even said. I thanked the men, Jude shook their hand, then each of the men took hold of the ropes and lowered the casket.

With a small concrete monument of a hound dog holding a basket filled with spring flowers in its mouth, the little pet cemetery became Maxwell's new home.

Getting over Maxwell was going to be tough. So when Bradley, a stockbroker who worked in the office next door, showed me a picture of a litter of four-week-old yellow Lab puppies, I just couldn't resist. And when I found out the litter of pups had been born on the very day we buried Max, I just had to have one of those puppies!

It was sort of like an omen, I thought.

After all, Labrador retrievers held the title of the number 1 dog breed, right? Well, that may be true, but I knew that trying to replace a beloved pet was the wrong thing to do. We just had to do it anyway.

So in February, we drove two hours on our thirty-fifth wedding anniversary to pick up Maxwell's replacement puppy. The litter had been born on a pig farm somewhere in western Illinois, just outside of a little town called Red Bud. "Somewhere" was right. Once we got into town, the rest of the directions were like this: Turn left at the fork in the road. Drive six miles down the gravel road. Make a right at the silo to the second farmhouse on the right. We never thought we'd ever get there.

Snow covered the ground, so we stayed inside and played with all the puppies right on the breeder's kitchen floor. I liked the little female with the colic on her nose, but Jude didn't like her for that very reason. No, he liked the little brute with a small black spot on his shoulder. So we handed the old man three hundred and fifty dollars cash and took our new little bundle of joy home.

Riding home in the truck, looking down at this sweet little pup curled up in my lap, stroking his soft new fur, I realized that I felt nothing for the little replacement puppy. I knew that we had made what was going to be a "big" mistake, and all I really just wanted to do was return him.

We felt so detached, and we couldn't even come up with a name for the poor little pup, so we just kept calling him buddy. He was a cute little guy, though. He could surf down the stairs on his little belly, he'd steal daddy's big ole shoes and put them with his own toys, and he would clear the sofa of all the throw pillows before finding just the right one to lay his head down on for an afternoon nap. Our new little puppy was definitely a little clown.

Our friends and kids would call on the phone. "Well, has he got a name yet?" they'd ask.

"Not yet, we still just call him buddy."

But every purebred dog should have a long, prominent name for its American Kennel Club registration, right? So we looked at his mom and dad's AKC papers to see if we could come up with a name based on the sire's and dam's names.

The dDam's name was Nellie of Dozer— . . . what is that?

His sire's name was Max something. Well, that was out of the question for obvious reasons.

Let's see, how about *Fisher*, because we like to fish.

And *Buddy*, because he'll be our fishing buddy. We'd been calling him buddy anyway.

Fisher Buddy and we'll call him Fisher.

The little guy finally had a real name. But Fisher never stuck. We had gotten too used to calling him buddy and so Buddy he would be. There was one exception though. Whenever Karie came home to visit, she would walk in the door and yell out "Hi, Fisher!" in a way that always got him going, racing around the house.

And Fisher didn't like to go fishing either. In fact, riding down the lake he would just try to hide under the boat seat. Have you ever seen a ninety-pound dog try to hide under something as small as a chair? And while we were fishing, he would just lounge on the back seat of the boat in the sun and wouldn't even move a muscle if a fish were caught. A real fishing buddy, all right.

Yes, Max and Buddy were two totally different dogs. In fact, if I had to describe the difference I would have to say that Max was my little boy dressed in a puppy suit and Buddy was the annoying little brother that I'd never had! And just to give you a few examples . . .

Shortly after graduating from his training crate to spending the day in our laundry room, one afternoon Lawrence, the carpet cleaner from my office, called to ask if he could stop by our house and refill the water tanks on his carpet cleaning truck.

"Sure," I said. But little did I know that was going to upset little Buddy.

From the garage, I walked into the house at the end of the day, and the very first thing I saw was the laundry room floor. The vinyl had been peeled like an orange, and the dog looked like he had just swallowed a canary. When Buddy heard Lawrence using the water faucet outside, he must have thought that Jude or I had gotten home and that he should be freed from the laundry room as we always did as soon as one of us arrived. Instead, he took his frustrations out on the laundry room floor. Yes, Buddy had peeled back the vinyl floor in the doorway a good two feet or so. After scolding him, I just threw a rug over the top of the torn vinyl floor, thinking that it was the first time he had ever destroyed anything in the house, but it probably wouldn't be the last.

By now, it was early spring, and one morning, I was dressed and ready to walk out the door on my way to the office. But before leaving the house, I decided to let the dog out. Buddy always just went out, took care of his business, and would want right back in the house, never wanting to stay out and play inside of the fence we had installed for him. I waited and wondered why he hadn't scratched at the back door yet.

"What is he doing out there?" I wondered.

Looking through the back-door glass, I could see him in the middle of the backyard with his big black nose to the ground, smelling something intently. I walked out onto our cedar deck and called, "Buddy, come!" But he didn't even look up at me.

In fact, I don't think he even heard me. He was mesmerized with whatever it was that he had found in the yard. So down the steps I clomped in my heels to see what the dog was so infatuated with. I was just a few steps away from him when he put his shoulder to the ground and began to roll on the unknown object, and then it hit me. The worst odor I have ever smelled in my life! One of the mallard ducks from the nearby pond behind our house must have laid an egg in one of the flower beds and guess who found it—Buddy! It wasn't just a broken egg either. I would catch a glimpse of the little embryo lying there on the ground every time Buddy would pick himself up and throw himself back down on top of it.

You've heard that expression "smelled like a rotten egg"?

Well, I've never smelled one before, but something tells me they don't smell like that. Words just can't describe how this smelled, but Buddy was covered in its stench. A hundred times worse than the foulest stinky foot odor.

The dog was mesmerized. He wouldn't, or maybe he just couldn't, come to me. I couldn't catch him, and if you want to know the truth, I really didn't want to. It was getting later and later in the day and I was late for the office! I stormed into the house, changed into my jeans, and grabbed my gardening gloves and the dog leash. I was bound and determined to catch this dog, armed with treats in one gloved hand and leash in the other, but the treats were no tradeoff for the broken duck egg. Besides, it was no use. I couldn't get close enough to the dog to grab him anyway because the stench was so overwhelmingly awful. I opened the fence gate and shouted, "Go swimming?" Labs do love the water. Buddy came barreling past me through the gate and headed straight for the pond behind our house and plunged in, letting him swim just long enough to rinse off. After that, we both needed a bath.

A few days later after letting Buddy back inside after doing his business, brown paw prints appeared right before my very eyes as he trotted through the dining room and into the living room. It wasn't mud either. He had stepped in poop! He circled back to the doorway of the kitchen.

"Come here, Buddy," I said in a melodious sweet voice.

In yoga position, "Downward dog." Buddy lowered his front legs, his butt went up in the air, and his tail began to wag frantically, and I knew I was in trouble.

"Buddy, come," I said slowly in a soft low voice.

With that, he ran toward me and jumped up as if to say, "Game on, let's 'play catch me if you can'!"

And with that, he tore right up the stairs. I knew better than to chase after him. I grabbed a handful of treats, opened the back door, threw them onto the deck, and Buddy followed his nose just as I knew he would. There were dozens of poopy paw prints in the dining room, through the living room, up the stairs, and down the hallway. Needless to say, I was late for the office again.

Then there was the morning after a sleepover for our grandkids. It was a nice fall day, and we were all in the backyard playing, Buddy included. Suddenly our four-year-old granddaughter, Abby, yelled out, "Ew!" Then grandson Ethan says, "Oh gross, a poop string!" And grandsons Alex and Evan began to laugh and point at Buddy. Jude and I looked at Buddy at the edge of the yard by the fence. A long, thin rope coated in diarrhea was dangling from his butt. Buddy had swallowed part of his toy, a rope tug. And about eighteen inches of it was dragging behind the dog. And since he was my dog, whenever he did something wrong, guess who had the pleasure of removing the remainder of the half-eaten rope tug?

By now, my annoying four-legged little brother was getting older and I was getting older too. He was four and I fifty-four. You know, going through those forgetful menopausal years.

Getting ready for the office in the morning, I laid my clothes out on the bed. Remembering something that I needed to do in the kitchen, I left the room. Passing the living room, I noticed Buddy doing what Buddy always did best, which was to lounge on his back on my white leather couch. All four paws in the air and with his ears turned inside out. After loading the dishwasher, I went back upstairs to finish getting ready for work. As I turned and reached for my pantyhose, they were no longer on the bed where I thought I had left them. Having misplaced things before, I became upset with myself and began the frantic search for the pantyhose, opening every dresser drawer, looking in the closet.

"Had I left them in the bathroom?" I asked myself. I hurried into the bathroom. Nope, not there.

"Maybe I left them in the other bathroom?" Not there either.

"I know, I must have left them in the laundry room when I ironed my clothes." No, not there either.

"This is making me crazy." I couldn't believe this was happening to me. After all, I thought that I was the most organized person I knew! I finally gave up my search for the misplaced pantyhose. I removed the ugliest pair of milky-white-looking pantyhose that I never wore from the drawer, except in case of an emergency, and this certainly was an emergency. After a long day at the office having to wear those ugly milky-white pantyhose, I pulled into the garage, closed the door, and walked into the living room. Lo and behold, there lay the misplaced pair of pantyhose smack dab in the middle of the floor.

"Buuuudyyyy?" I said in disbelief. "I can't believe this, you had my pantyhose the whole time. You made me think that I was going crazy!" I scolded Buddy.

But at the same time, a sigh of relief came over me. I wasn't crazy after all. Then I remembered that Buddy had a way of hiding things in the back of his mouth. He could put a pair of rolled-up crew socks in the back of his mouth, then grab a toy for a disguise, and you'd never know there was anything else hiding in there.

"He must have swiped the pantyhose that morning when I was preoccupied with loading the dishwasher," I thought.

That weekend, on Saturday morning, I was throwing something on just to run to the store to get some eggs to make breakfast. I had taken my pajamas off and laid them on the bed. I left the room for just a minute. I returned to my room to make the bed and put my pj's away, but my pajama bottoms were missing.

"What did I do with my pajama bottoms?" Once again, I instantly became upset with myself. "Where could I have put them?"

I rushed back into the bathroom but they weren't there. Then I remembered and stopped dead in my tracks. The pantyhose episode.

I yelled downstairs, "Are my pajama bottoms down there?"

"Yup, they're down here on the floor, right where Buddy left them."

I was relieved. But damn, he almost got me again!

"Annoying, annoying. Annoying little brother. This must be just like having a little brother!" I thought. And that's just the tip of the iceberg.

When we get home from work, it's impossible for Jude and me to have a conversation. As soon as we begin to talk to one another, Buddy gets between us and barks loudly. Except, if the subject is about ordering pizza, he immediately goes to the living room window to keep watch for the pizza deliveryman.

Relax on the couch and watch TV? Forget it. Buddy grabs his favorite toy and constantly tries to get you to play or will steal a sock right off your foot. As soon as you turn down the sheets on the bed, you'd better remove your pillow quickly or Buddy will have a great time humping it. And when he thinks it's time for you to get up in the morning, *grgrgrgrrrr*, he'll stare at you and growl softly until you finally do.

We would never be allowed at the dog park due to Buddy's natural ability to hump. The head, the tail, it didn't matter to him.

When we'd have a romantic moment, we have to close the door unless we want an audience.

Whenever Buddy want's his back scratched, he'll stand in front of you until you put your hand on his back, then he does a little jig with his back legs. You don't even have to move your hand.

He once ate an entire box of dog biscuits he found with the bags we had packed, ready for a trip to the lake. Needless to say, we were literally up all night walking the dog, if you know what I mean. And speaking of the lake, once the suitcases are packed, Buddy will sit with our bags just to make sure he doesn't get left behind.

And treats? If the treat you give him isn't exactly the one he had in mind, he'll spit it out onto the floor and look up at you with his whimsical big round eyes, waiting for you to give him another choice.

Display Christmas presents under the Christmas tree? No way. Buddy will unwrap every single one of them.

Fisher Buddy, our yellow Labrador retriever. Buddy may not be my little boy in a puppy suit as I used to describe his predecessor, Maxwell. But Buddy is what I always say Buddy should be—our dog.

An absolutely wonderful dog breed! Very intelligent, great retriever, loveable, quirky, a bit of a clown, and remain extremely large puppies until the age of five.

Now, at the old age of twelve, Buddy thinks he should have the last word. If he thinks that we've been watching TV too long or talking too much, he will growl and bark uncontrollably. And just like many humans, he doesn't approve of our texting or looking at our cell phones either.

With all that said, I wouldn't trade a Lab.

Twenty-six years, ranked number 1 breed in the US. Buddy doing what he loved to do best

Jude and Max sporting their sunglasses.

Buddy, the clown.

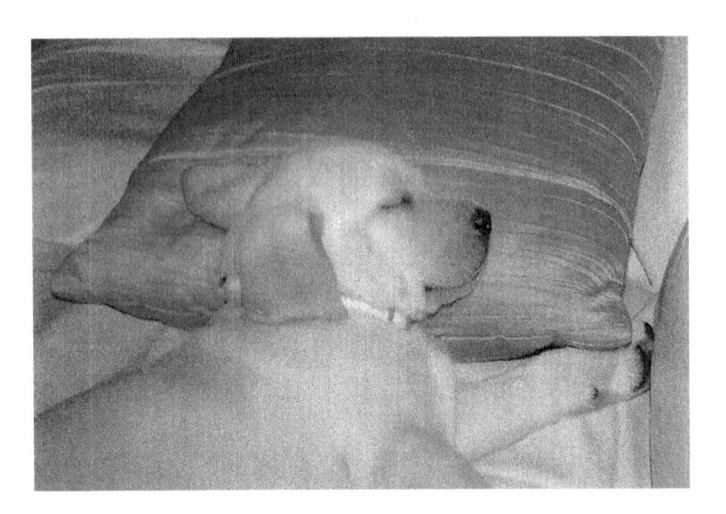

Buddy would clear the sofa of all the pillows before finding just the right one to lay his head down for an afternoon nap.

Abandoned

Over 100 years old and constructed of red brick, I had taken on the management of a one and a half story building in the historic district which had been converted into four small apartments. It was a hot summer day when I made my first visit to the property and was taken aback by the sight I saw on the wooden front porch. One of the residents was sitting on the steps basking in the sun. He was shirtless, a bit muscular, and had a huge snake draped over his shoulders… a Burmese python at least ten feet long! The man knew I was coming by to meet him, so I guess he thought he would try to shock me. Shock me he did! When a few months later I learned… on Christmas eve after abandoning his vehicle on a highway overpass to avoid police, he jumped to his death having miscalculated his landing. He was run over by several cars traveling down the interstate. Then, after the new year another tenant that lived in the old apartment building decided to move. It was the kind of day when the snow is beginning to melt when I arrived to do the moveout inspection. As I unlocked the back door, I couldn't help but notice little muddy paw prints in the melting snow and on the wooden door painted all white. The paw prints were unfamiliar to me as were the tiny droppings on the kitchen floor and the peculiar scent inside the apartment. Even after the door had been cleaned, the muddy little paw prints still appeared. I was locking up one morning after having shown the apartment and was stopped by one of the other residents. "Hey, did you know"? When those tenants moved out, they just turned their pet ferret's loose outside". "Awe, you're kidding", I said, "the poor things must be freezing, and they're still trying to get back in where they know it's warm. I keep finding more and more little paw prints on the back door every time I come to show the apartment"!

Enlisted to sell a small rental house on the west side of town that had been vacant for a few weeks, when I opened the basement door I couldn't help but notice the steps were covered in gray animal fur. I didn't think much of it, but felt it was a little chilly inside the house and I could see the access panel to the furnace was off and sitting beside it. I contacted my HVAC guy to have a look at the furnace. Rick was kneeling in front of the furnace when a cat flew right out of it and bounded across his back. The kitty had been there hiding inside the furnace. Well, eventually I successfully trapped the cat, brought it back to the office and my managers wife, Rebecca fell in love with the little abandoned critter and just had to take her home.

Ring, ring, ring. "Hello"? I answered the phone. "Hey, you're gonna have to get the snake out of this apartment before we can start painting it". Elliott, my painter said. "I saw it slither under the refrigerator when I walked into the kitchen"! He laughed.

Knock, knock, knock, the sheriff banged on the door of the house he was called to for an eviction. The door open's and the tenant said, "I'll just get my car keys". The Sheriff said, "Why don't you go get a moving truck, the movers may as well load a truck instead of putting your things out to the curb". The man replies, "There's nothing I want, I had my ole German Shepherd put down yesterday because I have nowhere else to go". With that, the man just got into his car and drove out of sight. It was upsetting to me that he could just have his pet euthanized instead of taking it to a "no kill" shelter! For days David, one of our maintenance workers tried to contact the man, leaving him voicemails that he would be happy to move his things to a storage facility or wherever he wanted them taken. The man never returned any of Dave's phone calls. So, David covered the belongings in heavy plastic to protect them from the rain and they remained there…abandoned, just sitting there at the curb.

In taking over the management of a duplex, I walked into what I thought was a vacant unit. Feces & used syringes covered the living room floor. When I entered the kitchen, I found a mixed breed puppy hunkered down under the kitchen table shaking like a leaf. I was able to find it a good home with my daughter's family, but one must wonder… how can people be so cruel, to just leave an animal locked up inside of a hot building with no food or water?

I was walking up the steps to an apartment for an eviction and the sheriff says to me, "It's bad in there". Piles of poop were everywhere in the tiny 4 room unit and the stench made my eyes burn! The tenants had moved out over a week earlier and had abandoned their two dogs and a cat which animal control had already came to rescue. You will learn a little more about these pet parents when you begin to read the last chapter and my story titled… "The Favor".

Me… Hello? "Hi this is Mark and the girl next door left her cat outside on the balcony for two days in the heat and I think it's going to die"! The tenant next door had been in the process of moving out, so I asked Mark to please give the cat something to eat and drink. The next morning, I would send Ronnie, my locksmith to rekey the door locks, then I would see what I could do about the cat. But, when Ronnie opened the door, the cat was now inside the townhouse! He did his best to try and corral it, but the cat somehow climbed up underneath the kitchen cabinets and Ronnie couldn't reach it. I phoned the tenant who had just moved out, "Hey, do you want to meet me at the apartment to help me catch your cat"?

"So, I'm supposed to be responsible for every stray cat in the neighborhood"? Jen said.

"Your neighbor told me that you have always had the cat", I replied.

"Nope, it's a feral cat, it's not my cat".

"Then what is it doing inside your apartment"? I asked.

I contacted county animal control. When the animal control truck arrived, Jen was just coasting up on her bicycle. I opened the door, Jen took one step inside and called the kitty by name. "Come here Mouzer". Crying, it came running to her. She scooped it up, gave it a kiss on top of its head and handed it to the animal control officer. As Jen handed the kitty to the man, she whispered, "I hope you find a new home, Mouzer". She then offered to donate her pet carrier to the animal shelter. A stray cat? I'm pretty sure it was yet… just another "Abandoned" pet.

Little House of Horrors

I could see her car with its unmistakable license plate frame resembling a heavy silver chain, pull up and park in front of my office. Joy, a middle age woman with long and unkept graying hair, would storm in to my office and toss her rent check at me. Sometimes landing on my desk, but often the check would just spiral across it, and down on to the floor. Then, without saying a word, she would spin around and storm right back out the door.

Joy had been a longtime resident of the townhouse when Gracie, an older lady, signed me up to take over the management of her 6 Family building.

When I would complain to Gracie about Joy's manners, she would always just say, "Oh I know! She's something else, isn't she"?

Hardly, how *"I"* would describe her…

One afternoon, I see Joy's car pull onto the parking lot. She flew into my office and threw her rent check down on my desk. As always, she spins around, and out the door she goes without saying a word. But this time, I see her open the door and rush back inside the office.

"Oh no! Here she comes back"! I thought.

"You want me to move, don't you!" she yelled at me.

Raising my hands up, as if to gesture…I surrender. I said, "Joy, that's entirely up to you".

"I'll just bet you do. Don't you!" she yells at me again. But, before I can utter a word, she storms right back out the door again.

"Geeze! What is wrong with that woman"? I said to myself.

A month or so after accusing me of wanting her to move out, Joy came to the office to pay her rent as she always did, but this time she was actually polite. She even placed her rent check in my hand instead of tossing it at me. Also, she gave me a handwritten letter explaining she would be moving out of her townhouse.

"I'm thinking…what in the world has gotten into her, she's really being nice for a change".

Joy said, "I'm always so sick, living here in Missouri. I've decided to move to Arizona where the weather will be a little better for me", she explained. "I can hardly breathe here, and I get a headache every day".

As soon as Joy turned in the keys to the townhome, I anxiously drove right over to inspect the unit, and man was I ever in for a shock!

I put the key in the front door lock and turned the knob, but the door wouldn't open. So, I shoved my shoulder and hip into it a couple times, and finally it opened.

Oh my gosh, the stench that hit me was enough to make me want to pass right out! No wonder Joy said she couldn't breathe and was always sick…who could live like this?

I closed the front door and couldn't help but notice the inside of it was rusted off at the bottom. "Then again", I thought. "I'll just leave the door open, so the place can air out a little".

The living room carpeting was soaked with urine, the steel front door not only was rusted off at the bottom, but the back door too. Suddenly, even *I* was getting a headache, so I went to the front door to get some fresh air. Having decided that I had seen enough of the place for one day, I just decided to head on back to the office to take some aspirin.

The next day, I decided to go back into the property. I noticed the wooden hall closet door was swollen at the bottom, and it looked as if it was wet. I took a piece of tissue from my bag to wipe it and see what it was. Holding the tissue to my nose, it was just as I thought… "whew, it was urine"! Joy's dog had been hiking its leg on *all* the doors in the house! "Well…that'll be enough for today", I thought. I was already getting another headache.

Next day, I at least made it to the kitchen to inspect the cabinets and appliances. That was all my head could take before it started hurting.

Day four. Up the stairs I go. As I passed one of the bedroom doorways, I was thinking, "Joy sure left a lot of furniture here for us to get rid of, and is that a real snake by that cat scratching post"? I stepped into the room to get a better look, "yep it's a real snake, alright". Time to go *now*! The little snake was dead of course, but I just couldn't take the pungent odor any longer.

Day five…do I really want to go to the basement? Before leaving the office to come to the apartment, at least I had the mind to take some aspirin *first*!

The smell emanating from the basement was a bit peculiar, a little different from the odor of the main and upper levels of the townhouse. There really wasn't much to see in the unfinished basement except lots of trash, so I walked across the concrete floor and opened the door that led to the single car garage. On the garage floor and right at the doorway, was the outline of what appeared to have been a dog. Poor thing must have died right there in front of the door. It had been left there long enough for its bodily fluids to begin to seep from it before Joy must have decided to get rid of it.

I slammed the door shut and thought I would vomit! Then heading back to the basement stairs, I caught a glimpse of something else from the corner of my eye and stopped to see what it was. Another outline of an animal! This one must have died under the staircase. I get a little closer and can see, it has white cat fur still stuck to it… AHHHH!

I barely made it up the stairs and out the front door. I quickly sat down on the front porch. I couldn't decide if I wanted to pass out, throw up or both!

Back at the office I called the owner of the building. "Gracie, have you ever been in Joy's apartment"?

"No, I guess not. Not since Joy moved in about eight years ago". she said.

"Woah, I said". "Well Gracie, we have a real mess on our hands. Every door in the place and all the carpeting *must* be replaced. All the subfloors will need to be sealed, and there was even an outline of a dead dog and a dead cat on the garage and basement floors. I even saw a dead snake up in one of the bedrooms"!

"Oh, my." Gracie said. "I didn't even know Joy had any pets".

Then it dawned on me. This was going to be a real problem.

Elliott, who had been my handyman and painter had recently moved out of state, and I hadn't found anyone to fill his shoes just yet.

So, a couple guys from my office, Bryan and Jason, decided they wanted to have a look at the property. They might give Gracie a bid and make a little extra cash, they thought. Well, needless to say… neither of them wanted any part of the place after seeing it with their own eyes (and noses).

In fact, none of the painters or handymen that went to the townhome to bid the job wanted to have anything to do with the place either!

I was finally able to talk Elliott in to…no, I BEGGED Elliott to come back to town and rehab… the *Little House of Horror's*.

The Irony of It All

The Salesman

How exciting! Do you remember how excited you were when you bought your very first brand-new car? That new-car smell and shiny new paint.

Exciting? At least that's what I thought. That is, until we began to shop for my first brand-new real estate car and our salesman went into a rage, and the paperwork wound up all over the showroom floor. Jude and I just looked at one another in disbelief.

I started my real estate career in 1976, driving a 1970 Dodge Dart Swinger. It was bright metallic blue, and it had aluminum wheels and two hood scoops on the engine hood. It was cool! But not exactly the type of car you'd want to drive clients around in.

Oh, there were other cool cars after that too. Like my 1976 Pontiac Le Mans Sport Coupe, which was really my very first real estate car but it was used, burgundy with a tan vinyl Landau top. Then there was the Cougar, as it was so fondly referred to by our son Jason's friends in the years to come, as they reminisced of taking it four-wheeling! This was truly my first brand-new car but still trying to cling to my youth, it was a bit sporty for showing real estate.

I'll never forget. We were on our way to the Lincoln Mercury dealer to buy it right off the showroom floor. Jude was backing out of the garage while I anxiously waited on the driveway when around the corner the very car we were on our way to buy—drove right past me and pulled onto the driveway across the street! Yes, someone our neighbors knew had bought our car! But all was not lost; the dealer promptly ordered another one just for us.

A bright red two-door with shiny spoke wheels, my 1986 Mercury Cougar was sweet. That is, until Jason and his friends got finished with it. It sounded like a diesel truck.

He was hounding us to buy a new car and dying to get behind the wheel of my old one. I didn't have a clue of what we'd even buy, but then have you ever been driving along, then a car fly's past you and you ask yourself, "What was that?" Then the next time you see it, you try to catch the name? Then finally you get close enough to make it out and quickly read the name on the trunk lid.

Then one Saturday morning, Jude spotted a newspaper advertisement from a dealership in the next county advertising "no haggle" pricing. Jason's sixteenth birthday was fast approaching and we were being pressured for the Cougar, so we decided to check out the add.

As we drove onto the new-car lot, we couldn't help but notice that all the prices were on every windshield in huge numbers, instantly revealing the "no haggle" price. And there it was, a shiny new 1994 four-door. Its silver paint shimmered so in the bright sunlight as if it were wet. Its big back seat seemed like that of a limousine, and its beautiful black leather interior had that great new-car smell. Then we took it for a test-drive, and it rode like we were floating on a cloud. It was love at first sight, and what a great real estate car it would be, and my first four-door too. In fact, my personalized license plates would be 1ST-4DR.

But Jude and I weren't ones to make an impulse buy, so we decided to go home and think it over.

As we were driving home, we decided to stop at our local dealer. After all, if we were going to buy a new car, why not keep the money in our own town, or so we thought.

Almost immediately, we spotted the exact same car on the lot that we had found at the other dealership with the "no haggle" pricing. We looked through the windows and looked it over real good on the outside, then we decided to go for it! If this dealer would even come close to our deal, we would buy this car right here, right now.

As we walked into the showroom, a tall thin man with dirty blond hair and wrinkled white shirt half-unbuttoned greeted us at the door.

"We'd like to make an offer on that silver new car out there on the lot," we said to the salesman.

"That one?" the salesman said as he pointed to my dream car.

"That's the one," I replied.

We then gave the salesman our offer and explained of how we had already swung the very same deal at their competitors and how we really just wanted to keep our money on this side of town.

"Well, okay," he said. "But my mother tried to buy that very car last week, and my boss wouldn't come down off the sticker price."

With that, the salesman walked up the stairs to his boss's office to present our offer. After a few moments passed, we heard the door slam loudly, then we saw the salesman come running back down the stairs, his face red with anger. As he stormed across the showroom floor toward us, we looked at one another.

I leaned toward Jude and whispered, "I guess his boss didn't like our offer."

As the man approached the desk where we had been patiently waiting, he gave our offer a toss just like he was throwing a Frisbee, right down onto the desk in front of us. The papers spiraled across the slick desktop before us, finally landing on the floor, scattering everywhere. Then without missing a step, he circled behind us and rounded the corner of his desk. He was so upset, he even knocked his desk chair over and onto the floor. He clumsily tried to pick the chair up but lost his grip and threw it back down on the floor.

"I can't believe this!" he shouted. "That fucker's gonna accept your offer."

Timidly I asked, "Is that a bad thing?"

"No! But my mom came in here just last week and made him the same offer and that prick turned it down!"

The man had already done everything wrong, but when he said, "I can't believe just anyone can walk in off the street and he'll take their money!"

I looked at Jude and said, "I don't know about you, but I'm going to get up and I'm going to walk out the door. I'm not going to spend nearly thirty thousand dollars on a car and be treated this way."

With that having been said, we both got up and marched right out the door.

Can you believe it? This salesman had a sale handed to him and then just let it slip away. He didn't follow after us. He didn't even make an attempt to apologize. We simply got into our car and drove away, and we never heard from him again.

You know that old saying? Hindsight is 20/20, whatever that means.

Well, let me just tell you what that means.

That means what we should have done that day was to have just swallowed our pride and bought that car anyway. But instead, we drove back to the other dealership and bought the first car that we had looked at. And that car turned out to be a lemon! The slang *lemon* refers to anything defective or broken or which breaks constantly and particularly my car!

In fact, whenever I would call to schedule an appointment for service, and when the service technician would ask, "What model is the car?"

"A New Yorker," I'd reply.

"What year is the car?"

"A '94."

"And what color is the car?"

"It's yellow," I'd reply.

He would always just chuckle because he knew that yellow was not an option and that it was simply just *that car*. That car. The one that got three new transmissions and two new air conditioners before it was even two years old!

Yes, if it just hadn't been for the salesman in his fit of rage, we would have bought the other car. The silver one.

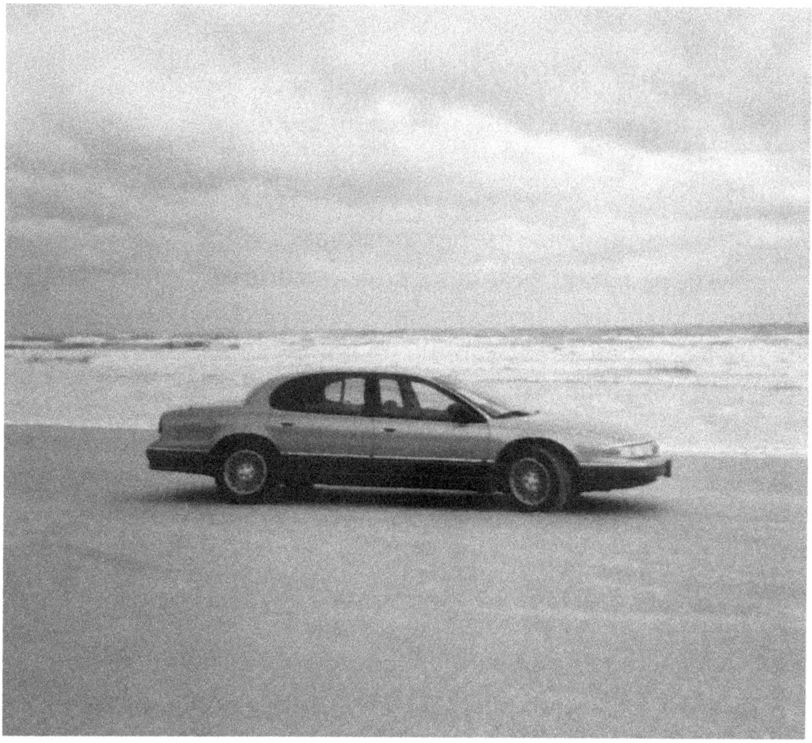

Road Rage

1ST-4DR, the personalized license plate of my very first brand-new real estate car, which also happened to be none other than my first four-door.

That shiny, sparkly silver paint with its "always wet" look, black leather interior, and oh, that new-car scent.

Never parking it near another car, and if you know me, then you know that's true. In fact, I can remember Douglas riding with me to meet a bunch of people from the office for lunch. When I pulled into my parking spot, Doug said, "What? Why are we parking way out here?"

"I'm not parking by all those cars."

"Why? It's just a car!" he said.

Despite of how anal I am about my vehicles, something always seems to happen.

Like the blue Dart Swinger getting front-ended by that guy with the crazy eyes driving a stolen car. My Mercury Cougar got bought right out from under me. My '04 Lincoln LS got hailed on just four months old with me standing in the doorway of the carpeting store, watching it get beat up. The bummer is that I had almost decided against leaving the office to return some carpet samples (it didn't hail at my office). Just two days old and our office building landscaper sprays freshly cut wet grass down the whole side of my brand-new Acura!

Back to my first four-door. If you're familiar of where my office is located, you'll know that it's a pretty busy road. Back in the day before the new overpass was built, traffic always backed up in front of the office.

It's the five o'clock rush hour. No different from any other day, traffic's backed up for nearly a block past my office. Everyone's just creeping along less than five miles an hour and there's finally a little break. The next car that's coming was a block away, so with just enough room to creep out and get in the line of traffic, I went for it. Almost to the highway, stopped in front of the building where our mail carrier found a dead guy while working her route some years later, it felt like my car moved but my foot's on the brake. Then it happened again. I looked in my rearview mirror and I saw a guy in the car behind mine and his face was expressionless. My car moved again, only now I was sure the guy behind me was nudging my car with his front bumper.

Being overly protective of my vehicles, I threw the shifter into P and jumped out of my car, leaving the door open. People in the other lane were rolling by, saying things like "He hit you" and "We saw him hit you." I was thinking, "Yeah, but I don't see you stopping to help me!"

So here I was, standing in the middle of rush hour traffic, with my dress and hair blowing all over the place. Flailing my arms, I stormed back to the guy's car and shouted, "You hit my car three times!"

With a degrading look on his face, he tilted his head and slowly said, "Get back in your car."

"No, *you* get *off* my car and why are you doing this?"

"You shouldn't have pulled out in front of me."

"Pulled out in front of you? You were a block away. I barely had enough room to inch out into the road, much less pull out in front of you!"

"I said get back in your car."

"And I said I'm not moving until you get *off* my car."

When I turned to walk back to my car, I noticed a magnetic sign on the driver's door with the name of a security guard company that I hadn't noticed before. By now, the traffic light had turned green, and there was no one in front of me, but I didn't budge. Horns were honking, people were getting out of line from behind the security guard car and speeding by. Finally, the big jerk put his car in reverse and went around me. I got the phone number from the advertisement plastered on both sides of his car and call the company.

"One of your security guards deliberately just pushed my car when I was sitting in traffic."

The gal on the other end of the line was very polite and apologetic to me and asked if there was any damage to my vehicle.

"No," I said, "but that guy's nuts. He's a loose cannon! Does he carry a gun?"

"Yes, ma'am, all our guards carry a gun."

Feeling a little sick to my stomach, I said, "You've gotta be kidding me. If I were you, I would take that guy's gun away before he goes postal on somebody!"

"Yes, ma'am," the voice on the other end of the line calmly said.

Well, that incident happened before *road rage* was called *road rage*, and now, twenty years later, would I dare get out of the car to confront a man that might have a gun? No way!

Cheater

The story has it that in December 1983, a singer from the St. Louis band known as Bob Kuban and the In-Men, a national success, went missing only to be found in 1987 stuffed into a cistern, which was located at the home of his shooter.

The singer had been shot in the back, and then dumped in a cistern on the shooter's property. Just two months prior to the disappearance of the singer, the shooter's wife of twenty-five years, was found clinging to life in her yellow Cadillac in a creek with the engine still running. she had been bludgeoned and deliberately driven into the creek. She was put on life support and then disconnected the very next day after CAT scans and EEG tests indicated that she was brain-dead.

I really had not heard much about the case, I never watched the local news broadcasts or read the newspapers, and to be honest, I was more into music like Pink Floyd's *Dark Side of the Moon*. I hadn't even heard of Bob Kuban and the In-Men when Robert, my manager, called me in to his office.

Mr. Meyer had just hung up the phone from talking with a local attorney who wanted an agent from our company to take a look at a property and to give a comparative market analysis to determine its value. I eagerly wrote down the address and said, "I'll take care of it."

A little later in the day, Robert came to my office and with a serious look on his face said, "You do know the story about this house, don't you?"

"Not a clue," I said. Then he filled me in, telling me the story and that this was the house where they found the body of the missing singer. I asked, "Why me?"

"Because they may need to rent the house if it can't be sold."

Creepy to say the least, I thought.

Scared to go to the house by myself, I enlisted my husband, Jude, to accompany me.

It was kind of a dreary spring evening in '88 when we pulled onto the driveway. The modest split-foyer-style home with its stained redwood front was located just outside of the tiny town of Cottleville in St. Charles County, Missouri. Jude turned off the ignition, we got out of the car, then we immediately noticed that lying a top of the retaining wall, which we had parked right next to, was a big Rottweiler that seemed to appear out of nowhere! The dog was just lying there, staring expressionless at the two of us, and didn't even move a muscle. We hurried into the garage, and when we turned around to look, the dog had vanished. "It was just there!" Needless to say, we didn't waste any time getting the garage door shut.

The Rot reminded me of the sneaky dog that lived at a house on the north side of town I had been watching to see if a tenant had moved. After knocking on the glass of the side door, I put the key in the lock and cracked open the door. Almost immediately, the dog jumped up on the door and thank God the door slammed shut. He was in the windowpane of the old wooden door pawing at it, growling, showing his teeth, and giving me the whale eye (when a dog shows the whites of its eyes), which in dog gestures means back off! You bet I did!

Already spooked, we entered the house with me cutting through the creepy cobwebs. The house had been vacant for a while, and there were dead bugs and thick cobwebs everywhere. Hurrying through the house, I became separated from Jude, then I heard, "Wooooooooooo." Jude thought he would be funny and make ghostly sounds, which bounced off the empty walls and echoed throughout the house. I knew the sounds were coming from him, but I hurried out the backdoor of the house where I became even more creeped out. There it was, the cistern that had been the singer's watery grave for four years. The very thought of it made me sick to my stomach. A local carpenter had even been hired to build a flower box on top of the cistern to hide it. A few years later, I learned that the carpenter had actually been one of my tenants that rented a house from me in Cottleville!

Back at the office, we came up with a fair market price for the property, and I was instructed to meet with the attorney.

At the attorney's office, it was explained to me that with the suspect in jail, I had to go to a relatives home to have the listing agreement signed. Unbeknownst to me, the shooter & the singer's widow were married and had been living where the murdered man had lived. To top things off, the house just happened to be in the subdivision where Jude and I had purchased a five-year-old home in 1982. How could we have not heard about this? Murder and lust right in our own backyard, so to speak. "We gotta get out more," I thought. Even more shocking was learning that they lived just two streets away from us.

I scheduled an appointment to meet. As I pulled on to the driveway in front of the white-frame and redbrick two-story, I noticed the home backed up to one of the subdivision lakes that Jude and I once had thought of building a house on. Sitting in the family room overlooking the small lake, I began filling out the listing agreement. As I was writing, I heard, "You know he was framed." Just hearing those five words felt like I was being pricked by a thousand tiny pins and needles. I didn't look up and I just kept writing. Again I hear, "You know he was framed."

I laid my pen down on the paperwork in my lap, looked up, and said, "I would rather not talk about it. I really don't know enough about the case."

Awkwardly, I finished working on the paperwork. I walked across the room, pointed where to sign, and was anxious to get out of the front door.

And so, the story goes the shooter was serving a life-prison sentence for the murders of his wife, and the singer, when he died at the age of seventy-two.

The Rottweiler wound up being the junk yard dog from across the road, and his owner purchased the house where the singer had been buried in the cistern.

I find the lyrics of the 1966 Bob Kuban and the In-Men pop hit with the man found in the cistern having been the lead singer of "The Cheater" … to be just a bit ironic.

Twelve Hour Day

Remember Margaret Raders rental house? And remember her tenants who had been away on a Christmas vacation? They had been such good sports when they learned their Holidays were about to be ruined… only to return home to find a sea of pink insulation covering the water soaked living room after a pipe burst during the night.

Well… before the "Happy Holidays" tenant, someone else lived at the rental house, which is how I met Margaret.

She contacted me about taking over the management of the rental property she'd been trying to take care of herself. She warned me of the couple that had lived in the house for many years. Apparently, they hadn't paid the rent for several months and Margaret just couldn't cope with it any more.

After mailing numerous late notices, making countless phone calls and taping notes to the front door, there had been no response from the tenants. And when they didn't show up for the court date, there was simply no other choice but to have the sheriff serve eviction papers. Even after the papers had been posted on the door by the sheriff, there was still no communication at all from the residents that lived in the house. In fact, they hadn't even bothered to rip the eviction notice off the front door the sheriff had plastered there with bright orange tape, a good 24 hours before.

The morning of the eviction, I arrived with the sheriff along with the moving company that Margaret had hired to move the tenant's personal belongings out of her house. The tenants rented moving truck was already backed up to the front door. I wasn't happy about the big box truck being parked on the lawn, but I was glad to see the tenants were at least making efforts to move. They were carrying armfuls of their belongings to the rented truck, but not one thing was in a box. Everything was being loaded into the moving truck piece by piece!

The sheriff and me agreed that it would be best if the movers could help load the truck. After all, the movers were being paid hourly and they were just standing around talking to one another. But the boss from the moving and storage company refused to let his crew help load the tenants truck.

"This is an eviction and all that stuff should be going out to the street", the boss said with disgust, as he pointed to one of the tenants who was carrying some of his clothes out of the house.

"Okay", I said. "Then go ahead and start moving things out to the curb".

The house was a smaller 1400ish square foot story and a half style home with a full basement, a double car garage and every square inch of the building was filled up. There wasn't going to be enough room on the moving truck for everything anyway because the tenants seemingly were hoarders.

The tenants continued to pick and choose what they did and didn't care to take with them. The movers just kept busy moving their belongings out of the house and setting them on the curb of the street. Only the curb quickly filled up with the tenant's things, from one edge of the property line to the other.

The tenants had everything they had chosen to take all loaded up on the rental truck and were gone now, or at least that's what we thought...

As the sheriff climbed into his unmarked car, he handed me his card. "I think I'm done here, call me if you need anything", he said.

I told the movers pretty much the same thing, and headed back to my office.

Shortly after lunchtime, I got a call from the moving company. "Just thought you ought to know, the tenant is back inside of the house rummaging thru everything", the man said.

"Thanks, I'll call the Sheriff", and I hung up the phone.

"Sheriff's department".

"Hello, this is Mrs. Jordan, and I just received a call from the moving company". "They wanted to let me know the tenants have come back, and they're inside of the house".

"I'm very sorry, but it's only the sheriff's job to stand by while the landlord takes possession of the premises", the Dispatcher explained. "We suggest that you contact the police department in the municipality where the property is located".

But when I contacted the city, I was asked if there had been an "altercation". I hadn't heard of any issues so far that day, and so they wouldn't send any help either.

"Looks like it's up to me", I thought. So, I drove back to the property.

I was taken aback when I pulled up in front of the rental. Earlier in the day when I left, there were household items and furniture that stretched from property line to property line and everything was out at the curb. Now the stuff not only covered the entire width of the property, but was also four rows deep, and stacked up a pretty good way up into the front yard!

I went inside of the house and told the tenant, "You need to go outside and let these men move the rest of your things out". "You can go thru your stuff as they bring it out and set it in the yard". The man shook his head, then reluctantly agreed and stepped out of the house and onto the tiny front porch.

I knew that I needed to stay there to stop the tenant from going back inside the house, so I was just wandering around the front yard, when…

Suddenly I heard the garage door fly open, and then immediately I hear it slam closed again!

"What do you mean, I can't take my damn car"! The tenant yelled.

The moving company boss got up in his face, "this is an eviction, and you're not taking that damn car anywhere"!

"WOHA, what do you mean he can't take his car"? I questioned.

"Because, I said he can't"! The boss then yelled at me, "this is an eviction"!

The two men began to push and shove one another. The tenant threw the garage door up and the boss slammed it back down, hard.

"Hey, take it easy on the garage door before you guys break it"! I shouted. Moving away from the scuffle, I quickly dialed 911. "Look, I have a situation at this eviction and you need to send an officer to this address *now*".

The car in the garage happened to be an old "Beamer" the tenant had been restoring. I knew the moving company boss was desperate to have it, because he had mentioned it to me earlier that morning. He said that he could apply for a Garage Keepers title, and sell it if the tenant didn't come to claim it.

The patrol car finally arrived, and the three of us met the officer as he slowly walked up the driveway toward us.

Before the officer had a chance to speak, I explained how there had been an eviction at the property that morning, and the tenant was trying to get his car out of the garage, but the movers wouldn't let him.

The officer looked at the tenant and asked, "will it start"?

The tenant shook his head, "no sir, but I can roll it down the driveway, and get it started".

Then the officer looked at me and said, "I guess it's up to this lady".

"If the man wants his car, I say let him have it"!

The boss just shook his head at all of us, and walked off in a huff.

The tenant didn't waste any time. He ran into the garage, hopped in his BMW, rolled it down the drive, and sped away.

Since everything seemed to be under control, I decided to slip back to the office to try to get something… anything, accomplished! It seemed like all I had done that day, was stand around or drive back and forth, up and down Interstate 70, from the office to the house and from the house to the office.

I was getting ready to go home for the day when I got a call from one of the neighbors that lived near the rental house.

"Are you the person in charge of this eviction that happened out here today"?

"Yes sir, I am", "my name's Nancy, how can I help you"?

"Nancy, can't something be done about all these people running around here"?

"Sir, what do you mean"?

"There are cars all over the place, and people are going thru the stuff that's piled up in that yard", the caller explained.

"Yes, I'll call the Police Department to see if there's anything they can do".

So, I called the city once again and was told, any property left at the curb is considered discarded, and I should have it removed as soon as possible. I already knew that. I was just asking for a little help…not a lecture.

It's seven o'clock in the evening! But here I go, back down Highway 70 for the umpteenth time to see what's going on at the rental house.

I pulled on to the dark street, and was in awe. There were cars everywhere. People were running up and down the street with their arms filled. All sorts of stuff strewn all over the yard, and even spilling out into the street.

As told by one of the neighbors… apparently the tenants that had been evicted earlier in the day, spread the word to everyone they knew, of where they could go to get all the freebee's they wanted!

Once again, I dialed the number to the Police Department.

"Dispatch".

"Hello"? "This is Mrs. Jordan, and I've called you a few times throughout the day, today". "Listen, it's eight o'clock at night, you've got to send a car here to break this up *now*". "People are running up and down the street carrying furniture & clothes from the eviction that we had here early this morning. Cars are parking on the wrong side of the street, people are yelling up and down the street to each other". "The neighbors are getting really upset, and this has got to stop! It's like a three-ring circus out here, plus it's getting late"!

"Yes ma'am, I'll send a car your way".

In just a few short minutes a patrol car rolled up, flashed its red and blue lights, hit the siren…*WHOOP, WHOOP*, and over the megaphone speaker mounted on top of the cruiser the officer ordered anyone that didn't live in the neighborhood to disburse.

It took a little while, but everyone finally left the area peacefully.

I waited until the last car full of people turned off the street and out onto the main road before calling it a day…a very, long… *TWELVE HOUR DAY.*

Action and Reaction

During winter months, whenever it's below freezing, I like to check on vacant properties just to make sure the heat is still working.

So I make the rounds checking on my vacant listings. One of which was a tiny house located on a rather large lot on the west side of town that I had listed for sale. As I put my key into the lock and crack the door open, I was certain that I could smell cigarette smoke odors emanating from inside the house. I went ahead and swung it open.

Strewn about the room were fast food bags and wadded-up burger wrappers, empty soda cups, beer cans, a burned candle sitting on a paper plate, and an ashtray filled with cigarettes sitting on the living room floor.

Quickly, I become spooked and quietly backed right out of the front door, tiptoed back down the steps, then ran as fast as I can back to my car!

I tried to call the seller who had moved out of the area, but there was no answer and no answering machine. Unable to leave the owner a message, I decided to call in the law.

"Emergency," the police dispatcher says.

"Hello, this is Ms. Jordan and I'm pretty sure that there is a squatter living in a vacant house that I have listed for sale."

I met the police car at the little house on the edge of town so I could let them in with the key. The officer threw open the door and yelled, "POLICE!"

The police officer was inside of the house for what seemed like a very long time and finally came outside to tell me that my suspicions were right and there was a man inside of the house. "He was asleep on the bedroom floor, passed out really. When I woke him up, he still seems to be drunk or something," the officer said. "I'm gonna check to see if there are any warrants out for his arrest."

The officer sat in his patrol car, talking on his police radio, then he went back into the house. A short time later, he and the handcuffed man that had been camping out in the house finally emerged.

With the man safely loaded into the back seat of the police cruiser, the officer approached my car. "This guy's really out of it, he can't really explain what he's doing here, so I'm just gonna take him to the station to sleep it off."

Later that morning, the phone rang and it was Vic, the owner of the house.

"Why in the fuck did you call the cops on my friend? I told him that he could crash at my house for a couple of weeks."

Well, that wasn't quite the reaction I expected. "Your friend?" I said. "I had no idea that he was your friend, you never told me that you were going to let anyone stay at your house, and I was trying to protect your property! What if another agent had gone to show the house to their buyer? There are food wrappers and beer cans all over the place, the house reeks of cigarette smoke, and your friend was passed out on the master bedroom floor."

"Well, I didn't realize he was going to wreck the house," Vic said.

"Well, he did, and please let me know if you are going to let him stay there again so that I can take the house off the market. We just can't show it the way that it looks and smells when he's there."

"Oh, it won't happen again," Vic said.

Not long after the house was cleaned up, an offer was received that the seller anxiously accepted.

In just a few short weeks, we were at the closing table and the first thing Vic asked to see was the new deed to the property. This seemed a bit unusual, but the closer at the title company was happy to oblige.

After reading the deed of trust for just a few seconds, Vic threw the papers down onto the closing table and said, "It ain't right."

The closer said, "It's just a standard form, sir."

"The legal description ain't right," Vic said.

"What's wrong?" I asked.

"Yeah, I'm not sellin' that whole fuckin' lot with that house."

Again, not quite the reaction I expected. "Well, what do you mean?" I asked. "You have never mentioned dividing the lot before."

"Well, I am sayin' it now and I'm not doin' it! I won't sell it unless I keep part of that lot."

"But, Vic, you would have needed to get the lot resurveyed, and we would have needed to disclose to the buyer that only a portion of the lot would be included with the sale.

"Screw that!" he said.

Mr. Ade, the closer and owner of the title company said, "Sir, I'm going to have to ask you to refrain from using that kind of language in my office."

Vic apologized and agreed to watch his language.

An hour and a half had now passed. The closer and I were not having any luck trying to make the seller see that he just didn't get to decide on the day of closing that he got to keep part of the lot.

So I decided to call in the big guns, Donald M., who was the owner of the company at that time, to please come down to the title company to try to reason with this seller.

Donald arrived about a half an hour later, sat, down and began to explain to Vic that keeping a portion of the lot would just not be that easy. "First, do you know if the neighborhood restrictions will allow subdividing the property? If so, you'll need to pay for a survey to divide the lot. There will be recording fees and the buyer will need to agree, as will the buyers loan company. There would most likely need to be a new appraisal, and with less lot square footage, the property may no longer be worth the contract price. There are other things to consider too. The buyer and the selling company could sue you for not consummating the sale. Why, we could even sue to collect our commission. I don't think we would do that, but I can't speak for the other company."

"Sue?"

That magic word. Once Vic found out that he stood nothing to gain by trying to hang on to a portion of the lot, he decided it would be better to close the deal than face a possible lawsuit.

It seemed that Vic had come with a plan to renegotiate the deal right at the closing table. Before finally realizing his plan wasn't going to work, it took about four hours and one magic word to change his mind.

I'd like to take this opportunity to thank my Meyer family. I wouldn't be where I am today without them, leastwise I wouldn't be writing these memoirs. Thank you!

What the Hail!

In the spring of 2016, the Midwest had its fair share of stormy weather.

I was busy trying to figure out which of the properties I managed that had been in the path of the storms, might have been damaged, and was contacting local contractors to assess the damages. Some of my owners had already taken it upon themselves to contact some of the local contractors, and Connor was one of them.

Connor lived back east and was handling things long distance. He had actually done a pretty good job and had gotten things taken care of a little cheaper than I could have. The downfall of an owner taking care of business themselves is that sometimes I get left out of the loop. How am I or the tenant to know who and when someone is going to be on the property working?

So when a man came to Kay's door and said that he was there about the siding, she didn't think a thing of it.

After all, the neighbors were all getting new roofs and siding, and the subdivision was buzzing with all kinds of insurance adjustors, roofing, and siding trucks every day and unfortunately a few storm chasers too.

In this case, storm chasers are just companies that flock to areas that have unfortunately been hit hard by tornadoes, floods, and wind damage, and our area had been hit pretty hard by a couple of hailstorms. Some storm chasers are legitimate and some are just rip-off artists.

Speaking of storm chasers, a few years ago back in 2012, there were bad hailstorms which brought a lot of unfamiliar contractors to the area. One roofing company in particular had rented a three-bedroom, two-story-style home from me. The home was located in a quiet court where the owner had once lived, and of course, he had known all the neighbors. The roofing company was based in another state, and the house had been rented to the owner of the company and his brother. Everything seemed to be on the up and up until I received a phone call from, the landlord, after a few months had passed.

"Hey, Nance, it's Ben. Yeah, one of my old neighbors called me this morning and said that he thinks there are more people living in the house than there should be. Yeah, he said that there are at least ten guys living there and maybe even more! Said he wouldn't even know there were so many people there because they leave early in the morning and don't come back until after dark, but then after they get home, most of them kick back and have a few beers in the garage every night. They're quiet, I just didn't think that you would want that many people living in your house," the neighbor explained.

"Wow, Ben, I'll talk to my manager and we'll check it out ASAP," I said.

Early in the morning, my manager Doug and I went to the white two-story with keys in hand to check things out.

Neither one of us had ever seen anything quite like it before. The house was really pretty neat and orderly, but nearly every room had mattresses on the floor or cots set up. There was even a stack of foam insulation on the hearth of the fireplace with blankets neatly stacked at the foot of the makeshift bed. All of the so-called beds were either nicely made up or had been stripped, with sheets and blankets folded and neatly placed at the foot of each bed. All in all, we counted twelve sleeping areas, but the house, much to our surprise, was clean.

After checking the house out, we called Ben and told him of what we had found. I was a little surprised when Ben just laughed and said, "Well then, I guess they can stay as long as they're takin' care of the house and stay quiet."

So I contacted the owner of the roofing company to let him know that we were on to what they were doing and that we had inspected the house and had seen for ourselves, the evidence of so many people living there.

He assured me that none of his men were criminals and that they wouldn't bother the neighbors anymore by hanging out in the garage and agreed to pay what the lease called for which was *double* of what the stated rent amount was on the lease agreement.

Several more months passed, and once the work in the area ran out, the roofing company paid a substantial lease break penalty and moved out, leaving the house clean and in good condition.

Knock, knock, knock. Kay opened the door and there stood the man that had told her two hours earlier that he was there to look at the siding.

The man was speaking broken English but somehow Kay managed to understand enough to know that he had removed all the siding from the side of the house and was asking her to open the garage door so that he could put the siding that he had removed from the house inside of the garage.

Not communicating very well, the man just couldn't understand Kay's objections to what he had done, so she asks to speak to his supervisor.

Turns out the man had removed the siding from the wrong house! All the siding had been removed from the west side of the house and there was nothing but bare wood covering the garage.

The supervisor apologized profusely and promised to make it right and that they would be right out to put a tarp on the side of the house.

Kay said that Connor was going to contact the company, and luckily Kay had the peace of mind to take a quick photo of the work truck. Like I said, I had been left out of the loop, so I just allowed the owner to handle things, but it wasn't long and I couldn't help myself and just had to get involved.

I spoke to Connor, who explained that he was losing his patience and wasn't getting anywhere with these guys. "Nancy, they keep telling me that they can't find the siding and that they will take care of it. They haven't even put a tarp on the house yet, so it's all exposed!"

I asked Connor for the names and phone numbers that Kay had given him—Carl, Al, and Ken—but there were only two phone numbers that worked.

Carl answered, but I couldn't understand a word he was saying, nor could he understand me, so he handed off the phone to Al. It was rough, but I managed to find out that it was Ken that I needed to speak with.

After several phone calls and unanswered messages, Ken finally answered.

"Hi there, I'm calling about the house that you mistakenly took the siding off," I said.

"Do you mean that I can talk to you? I would like to talk with you from now on. That owner, Connor? He is being very mean and I don't want to talk with him anymore, that's why I won't talk to him."

"Well, understandably so, I can understand why Connor is upset. You took the siding off his house over three weeks ago, and we still don't even have a tarp on it yet. It's just bare wood!"

Ken agreed to put a tarp on the house that day but told me that he could only find one box of that type of siding and that he needed two boxes.

We kept in contact with each other every week. I asked if he had found another box of siding and he told me that he just might have found another box. It wasn't but a few weeks later and I found that Ken's phone had been shut off. I tried Carl's number and the mailbox was full.

With nothing left to do, I contacted the local police and met Officer Ledder at the property. I gave him a photo of the truck that Kay had taken, which had a fuzzy image of the license plate, but I wasn't very encouraged by what the officer had to say.

The license plate was traced to a woman in another state, but she claimed to know nothing.

Eventually, Connor gave up on getting the trio to replace the siding on his house that had been mistakenly removed and filed an insurance claim on the missing siding.

Can you imagine someone just taking the siding off your house? I'm sure you would say exactly what I said—what the hail!

Kay had the peace of mind to take a
quick photo of the work truck.

There was nothing but bare wood covering the garage.

The Favor

One of the things I've always enjoyed about my real estate career was being able to help people out, and if anyone needed my help, it was Nicholas.

Nick was a tall middle-aged man trying to self-manage a small apartment complex on the edge of town. He had appointed one of his tenants to be a resident building manager, but the only managing this tenant had done was to make a real mess of things.

Armed with a stack of file folders tucked under his arm and a big yellow envelope in his hand filled with keys that jingled when he walked, Nick had come to my office with a plan in mind, confident that he was going to hire me to manage his apartment buildings. After a long conversation with Nick, I managed to discover that a few of the tenants were so far behind on the rent that they needed to be evicted, including the so-called resident building manager.

I thought to myself, "The buildings aren't in the best location, they're run-down, there were derelict vehicles all over the parking lots, half of the tenants aren't paying the rent, and some of them even need to be evicted. No thanks, mister."

Then I said, "Nick, I'm really sorry. But I just don't think I would be interested in managing your properties."

"But why wouldn't you be interested?" Nick asked.

"Why? Well, there's just too much work to do just to get things back in order again before we can even begin to manage these properties."

Nick looked at me with his big blue eyes, leaned toward me, and said, "I really need your help. Please, is there anything I can say to change your mind?"

And that's all it took. I could tell that he desperately needed my help, and I was a sucker for those blue eyes.

With that, I agreed to take on his properties. Nick anxiously handed over all his thick file folders and the big yellow envelope filled with keys to all his units, and just then, it hit me and I thought to myself, "I must be crazy."

Then the nightmare began. My very first task was to have the proper tow signs installed on the property and place tow stickers on the unlicensed vehicles before having them towed from the parking lots and to begin eviction proceedings on the building manager, among many other things. The common area basements were just filled with abandoned items left behind from tenants past. Old headboards, mattresses, tires, trash, and did I mention cobwebs so thick that you could cut them with a knife?

My first target was an old beat-up gray pickup truck, checking the appropriate boxes—unacceptable condition, check; unlicensed, check; date to be towed, check. I plastered the bright green tow sticker on the driver side window of the gray pickup and then returned one week later to see if it was by any luck, gone. The truck had been moved to another parking spot and traces of the green tow sticker dotted the window where it had been torn from the glass, but the truck was still there. How exciting, I was going to get to tow my first vehicle, so I called the number of the towing company that was printed on the sign and requested a tow.

A flat bed wrecker was there within minutes. After jockeying the truck from its parking place with tires screeching, the tow truck driver pulled it up onto the bed of the wrecker. The old gray pickup was gone and I was back at my desk in no time.

Within fifteen minutes, the phone rang and it was the former resident building manager.

"Where in the fuck is my fuckin' truck?" he shouted.

Calmly I explained, "You can call the number on the sign and pay the tow bill and storage fees to claim your truck, but don't bring it back or it will just get towed away again."

"Just who in the fuck do you think you are? Towin' my fucking truck." He questioned again. "Look, all you did was tear off the tow sticker and move the truck to a different parking spot, when you could have at least called me to try to work something out." I explained.

With that, the building manager had a few choice words to say to me, which I am just sure you can imagine, and then he slammed the phone down in my ear.

Next on the agenda, the eviction. Although the apartments were located within the city limits, it's always the county sheriff's duty to post the eviction notice, give the landlord possession of the property, and keep the peace during the process of placing all personal belongings at the curb of the street. Boy, did I ever need law enforcement that day and keep the peace? That was putting it mildly.

When I arrived at 9:00 a.m., the sheriff was already there, my new locksmith and comedian Mr. Benne had already picked the lock and had the door open, and the sheriff had already called for animal control's assistance. When animal control officers arrived, they rounded up two dogs and a cat from the apartment. It appeared the animals had been abandoned there.

As I was walking up the stairs that were located on the back of the building to the second-floor unit, the sheriff was just stepping out the door and onto the tiny balcony.

"It's bad in there, you might not want to go in," he said.

"Just great." I scowled as I stormed past him and went through the door to the kitchen.

The second I stepped inside the door, it hit me. The stench of feces and urine. The smell was so strong that it made my eyes water and gave me an instant headache and was enough to gag me.

As told by the neighbors, Derrick and Jill had been staying with friends across town, but they hadn't taken their animals with them.

The carpet looked like a minefield of poop and was soaked with urine. I literally had to tiptoe between piles of poop to look at the apartment. As I looked around, I couldn't help but notice the ceiling was painted black, and every wall was painted a different primary color, dark blue, bright red, and yellow. Certainly not my taste, but then again neither was living in filth either.

Fanning his hand in front of his nose, the sheriff said, "I've never seen one quite this bad before."

"Me neither," I shouted.

I looked at David, my maintenance man, and ordered, "Get everything out of here and onto the curb and take the carpet and pad out too. This is a disgusting mess."

"Oh, why am I even here?" I thought. I knew I shouldn't have said yes to Nick. Just then, a young woman in her early twenties emerged from the bedroom where she must have been hiding in the closet or under a bed.

"And just who are you?" I asked.

"My name is Dawn and I don't have anywhere else to go. I'm homeless and Jill said that I could stay here." She sobbed.

"You're living here? In this filth?"

"I didn't have anywhere else to go," Dawn said as she looked down at the filthy living room carpeting.

Unbelievable, I thought. But oh, it gets even better.

Just then, with her five-year-old daughter in her arms, Jill came busting through the back door to the apartment. "What in the fuck do you people think you're doing here?" she shouted.

"You know exactly what we're doing here. I'm the sheriff."

Waving a piece of paper around in front of Jill's face and pointing to the door, the sheriff said, "I posted a copy of this notice on that door twenty-four hours ago. Now you need to leave the premises and your things are going to be taken out to the curb."

Jill began to scream, "Where are my fucking dogs? I love those fucking dogs!"

Looking down at the minefield of poop and with a hint of sarcasm I said, "Oh, we can see that."

Jill stood her daughter down on the kitchen floor and glared at me. "Fuck you. What did you do with my fucking dogs?"

"They've been taken to the city pound and you need to lose the language," the sheriff said.

Stepping over the poop, she took the little girl by the hand and walked into the living room.

Pointing to the girls little bare feet, the sheriff shouted in his booming voice, "Where are her shoes?"

"I didn't have fuckin' time to put them on 'er because I heard that you fuckers were in my apartment."

"You had time to put your shoes on," he said.

"It's cold outside and there's snow on the ground," she explained to the sheriff.

"*Exactly,*" he yelled at her. "Get her out of here before I call Family Services," he barked.

Jill picked the little girl up and took her outside, leaving her in the care of the homeless girl. But it wasn't long and she was right back inside running her mouth again.

Jill was rifling through the things in the bedroom and screaming, "I can't believe these fuckers, they took my fucking dogs away, they're putting my fucking furniture on the street."

Sheriff said, "Look, I told you, lose the language or I'm gonna throw you out."

"This is fucking ridiculous, you fuckers think you can come in here and—"

"Out! I told you to shut your mouth. You shouldn't be in here anyway. This is an eviction. Go outside now and I don't want to hear your mouth again or I'll find a way to have you escorted somewhere . . . away from here."

Jill stormed out of the front door, ran to the street, and began going through her things. Every sentence that came out of her mouth was f—— this and f—— that. The sheriff was sitting in his car talking on his radio, then he walked up to me and said, "A car will be here to pick her up shortly. There's an outstanding warrant for her arrest. I warned her to shut her mouth or I'd find a way to get rid of her." Not long after, two Wentzville police cruisers rounded the corner and the sheriff approached Jill.

"You're being arrested on an outstanding warrant. Do you have someone that can pick your daughter up?"

"You have got to be fucking kidding me. You throw me out of my apartment and now your fucking arresting me?"

"Hey, I told you, lose the language. Do you have someone that can pick her up?" The sheriff pointed to Jill's little daughter. "Or do I need to call Family Services?"

Jill began to cry. "She can take her." She pointed to the homeless girl.

The sheriff looked at the homeless girl. "Who, her? Why, she doesn't even have a place to go, and do you even know her? No. You need to call someone else to come and get your daughter or I'm calling Family Services."

Jill dialed the phone. Sobbing, she said, "Hey, I'm fucking being arrested, so can you come pick up my kid or they're gonna fucking take her away from me."

Rolling our eyes and shaking our heads as we listened to Jill's conversation, the sheriff and I just looked at one another.

As soon as Jill's friend drove out of sight with the little girl, Jill was handcuffed and put into the back of one of the waiting police cars.

The sheriff and I both sighed a sigh of relief. Finally, some peace and quiet.

Dawn, the homeless girl, was just sitting on the front porch. With nothing left to do but wait for the guys to finish setting Derrick and Jill's things on the curb, I joined her on the front porch steps to get some fresh air.

"Where will you go now?" I asked.

"I don't really have anywhere else to go," she replied.

"What about the Salvation Army? Why don't you go there?"

"I guess I could try."

"Are those the only shoes that you have?" I asked her. She was wearing a worn-out pair of flip-flops.

"Yeah." She looked down at her foot, moving it around in a circular motion as if to admire her worn-out sandal.

"I'm sure there are shoes out there at the curb. Why don't you go see if there is anything there that will fit you? I don't think your friend Jill would mind."

"No, that's okay, I love wearing flip-flops. Besides, she wasn't my friend, she just said I could crash here."

"But there's snow on the ground," I argued.

"That's okay, it doesn't bother me."

With that, she hopped to her feet and asked, "Now where is that Salvation Army place?"

I gave her directions and she was on her way.

"Can I drop you off there?" I yelled to her.

"No thanks, I like to walk," she shouted back.

For days after the eviction, the neighbors reported that Derrick and Jill just kept coming back to the building and taking things from the common basement. One day, I had even seen Derrick slip behind an old mattress to hide from me! And I just kept calling the police. They finally stopped coming when the police threatened that they would be arrested for trespassing if they entered the building again.

I've said it before and I'll say it again—what have I gotten myself in to?

Which brings me to the next item on my agenda.

Sheila. A middle-aged woman who had written Nick a bad check for her security deposit and her first month's rent. After weeks of never being able to collect the rent or security deposit, we finally received a default judgment against Sheila. She just didn't show up for court. So the sheriff posted an eviction notice on the door after the ten-day waiting period was up. The twenty-four-hour notice was posted by the sheriff late in the day on a Friday afternoon, stating that he would be back bright and early on Monday morning at 9:00 a.m.

Most tenants are only given a twenty-four-hour notice of an eviction, but even though Sheila had been given the entire weekend to move, she was still in bed on Monday morning when we arrived.

Bang, bang, bang, the Sheriff beat on the front door. "Sheriff's Department," he yelled through the door. But there was no answer. Then around to the back door we walked through the deep snow that had fallen the night before. *Bang, bang, bang,* he pounded on the door. No answer. He then told the locksmith to drill out the lock. Just as the locksmith began to drill the lock, Sheila peeked out from behind the curtains. She was still half-asleep.

The door opened. "What do you want?" she asked, squinting her eyes from the bright morning sun reflecting off the white snow-covered parking lot.

"Sheriff's Department, you're being evicted this morning."

"Evicted? But I didn't get any notice," Sheila sleepily said.

"Ma'am, I personally posted your eviction notice not only on this door, but your front door too on Friday afternoon. So you not only got a twenty-four-hour notice, which is what most people get, you got the whole weekend to move out!"

"Oh, but I don't have any boxes or anything. Can I have just a few more days?"

"That's up to your landlord, ma'am."

They both looked at me. I was bouncing up and down just trying to keep warm. The snow was coming down again and it was freezing cold.

I shook my head. "No way, your deposit and rent check both bounced, you don't return phone calls, you made us take you to court, you didn't show up, you've had the entire weekend to get out, and I'm not leaving here today until you are gone."

The sheriff looked back at Sheila, tilted his head to the side, and said, "You heard the lady."

"Well, can I at least go get a truck," she asked.

"You can go do anything you want to, but we're going to go ahead and start cleaning out the apartment."

"But I don't have any boxes."

"That's not my problem, you had the whole weekend to get boxes. These men are being paid by the hour and they're not just going to stand here and have coffee for the next hour while they wait for you to get back here with a truck."

Donald M., the previous owner of the company that I worked for, had stopped by just to see how things were going. He said, "Oh,

I think we can wait for the truck, can't we? Or maybe even another day?" Oh, he was just such a softie.

But I had been chasing this woman for weeks. After numerous unreturned phone calls and unanswered letters, I was extremely mad at this woman that I never even met or had even talked to.

"No way, it has taken us two months just to get to this day, and we're not about to start over again because you did nothing about renting a truck or even packing a single box." With that having been said, I told the movers to get started.

Sheila left to go rent a truck, and the movers began bringing out stacks of dishes, pots, and pans, and as soon as the men would set them down on the snow-covered parking lot, they would begin to slide away. Everything was nearly out of the apartment except an antique piano when the moving truck arrived, and since it was the last thing left in the apartment, it was the first thing to go on the truck. As the men pushed the piano through the snow-covered parking lot, the piano keys began to cling and clang in an off-key sort of way. I just shook my head in disbelief.

"What on earth was this woman thinking?" Better yet "What am I even doing here!"

Then there was Phillip. He had been displaced by Hurricane Katrina, or so he claimed. If you will remember, Hurricane Katrina hit the Gulf Coast on August 29, 2005, and oddly enough, Phillip moved into his new apartment in Missouri on August 1. Yet somehow he still managed to receive monthly payments from FEMA. He was a bit odd to say the least as you will soon learn. Yes, Phillip was from somewhere in the bijou all right and he had a heavy accent to prove it, but I had my doubts about his being one of Hurricane Katrina's victims. He was a nice-looking guy with sandy brown hair and was an electrician by trade. I wondered why Phillip just never seemed to be able to hold down a job, but after getting to know him a bit better, it all became clear as mud to me.

The first time I met Phillip, he had come to my office to pay his rent in person as many tenants did. While I was writing out his rent receipt, I could feel his eyes looking at every inch of me. Feeling very uncomfortable, I glanced up at Phillip and our eyes met.

"Is that still in force?" he asked.

"Is what in force?"

Then he put his finger on my wedding ring and rolled it from side to side.

I quickly pulled my hand away and rested it on my lap under the desk.

With a puzzled look on my face, I said, "Yes, it is very much in full force and effect, thank you."

Wow! What was this guy thinking? That I would be interested in the likes of him? He who can't hold down a job, who is ripping off the government, who hardly had anything to his name and rents a cheap apartment from me?

I knew that this was going to be an interesting experience right from the get-go.

It was the beginning of the New Year and Phillip, who was always out of a job, came to ask if the landlord had any work that needed to be done because he did not have enough money to pay the January rent.

We did have a vacancy that was in need of some painting, so I contacted Nick for permission to let his tenant work off some of the rent.

"Hi, Nick, it's Nancy."

"Oh, wow, it's never good whenever I get a call from you." Nick laughed.

"No, don't worry, it's nothing. In fact, we have the vacant apartment rented and your new tenant will be moving in the first of February. It's your tenant, Phillip. He says that he's low on cash and doesn't have enough money to pay this month's rent, but he's looking to trade some painting on the vacant apartment in exchange for the rent on his apartment."

"I've seen his work and he does a good job. Sounds good to me, so let him go ahead and get started," Nick replied.

And so, with the landlord's blessing, Phillip was given permission to get started on the apartment.

After checking in with Phillip from time to time to see how things were coming along, he would always say that everything would be done on time. Well, it was nearing the end of January and the week just before moving day, so I decided to drop by the apartment on my way to the office on Monday morning.

As I opened the door, my jaw dropped. Phillip had not touched the apartment. There wasn't even a paint can or paintbrush in sight, and Phillip was nowhere to be found either. After all, Phillip had assured me time after time that things were moving right along.

Panic came over me. I had exactly six days to get the apartment painted, cleaned, and carpet-cleaned and get it to pass a city occupancy inspection.

As I dialed my cell phone to call the painter that I normally used, I hurried to my car, all the while wondering why I had let Phillip talk me into letting him work off the rent.

"Elliott!" I shouted. "You won't believe this, but the tenant we gave that paint job to just to help him out on his rent. He has not even made a brushstroke in the unit and I only have six days left to get this apartment ready for the new tenant who is moving in on February 1. Help!"

El just laughed. "Hell, I figured this would happen, so I've been planning all along that I might need to drop everything and go paint the place."

"Oh, thank you, thank you. Thank you."

At the office, I unloaded my arms and sat down at my desk, and before even taking my coat and scarf off, I was dialing Phillip's number.

After about the tenth ring, he finally answered, "Heeelloooo?" He sounded groggy.

"What are you doing!" I shouted into his ear.

"What's the problem here?" Phillip softly asked.

"What's the problem? You have had all month to paint that apartment, there are only six days left before a new tenant moves in. I still have to get it cleaned and the carpet cleaned and get it inspected by the city!"

"No worries, I'll get it done," replied Phillip.

"No way, forget about it. I have already hired another painter."

"But we had a deal, you said I could paint the apartment so I wouldn't have to pay this month's rent."

"Yeah, but you didn't paint the apartment and I simply can't wait any longer."

"Where I come from, people don't go back on their word. Guess you people 'round here don't care about things like that. See it every day."

"Well, around here, when I give someone a job, I expect them to do it. You will just need to figure out another angle to get your rent paid. I'll let you go now so you can go back to sleep." Then I just slammed the phone down.

That's all it took. From then on, Phillip was full of outrageous antics toward the other tenants and guess who? Yours truly.

Quickly I began to know why most working people just don't like Mondays.

The message light on my phone was on and flashing that there were ten messages. Two of them were from tenants that resided at the small apartment complex.

The first message was from the older woman who had just moved into the newly painted apartment.

"I don't know what kind of place I just moved into, but that man they call Phillip? Well, yesterday he put a television set on the tailgate of his truck and sat outside with the snow coming down, watching TV and drinking beer."

The next message was from Brian, one of Phil's drinking buddy neighbors.

"Yesterday afternoon, Phillip had an electrical cord strung across the parking lot to a TV propped up on his tailgate, watching the game, and every time somebody would run over it, Phil would jump out of his chair, shake his fist, and cuss at 'em. I just don't want him to get evicted, that's all."

It was Super Bowl Sunday, snowing outside, and a perfect day for the game. Guess that was Phillip's version of "tailgating?"

I called Phillip to tell him not to do anything like that again, but he didn't seem to think there was anything wrong with what he had done.

"What? You mean a guy can't kick back, have a few beers, and watch the game at his own home?" Phillip asked.

"IN, your own home, Phillip, not on the parking lot, and you were yelling and cussing at the other tenants and tossing your beer cans and cigarette butts all over the place."

"Well, it's a pretty cold day in this country when you can't even watch a football—"

"Phillip, stop! It wasn't an acceptable thing to do and just don't do it again." I hung up the phone.

That was just the first of many, many more of Phillip's shenanigans.

He loved to poke a broomstick handle on the floorboards from below the basement of the first-floor apartments early on Saturday and Sunday mornings. When I say early, I mean 6:00 a.m. He had probably been up all night drinking and hadn't even been to bed yet. When asked what he was doing, he would reply, "Just doin' my job, workin' for the real estate company."

He was also known to go into vacant apartments while other vendors were there to give estimates for work to be done. He would walk around with a clipboard, writing things down. When asked what he was doing, he would reply, "Just workin' for the real estate company."

One afternoon, Phillip's neighbor and so-called friend Brian stopped by my office to pay me a visit.

"Yeah, I don't want Phil to get evicted or anything like that but last night? Last night he broke into my apartment in the middle of the night. He was drunk and I had to fight him all the way out the door. I was tryin' to get him down the stairs, but he wouldn't go and then finally we scuffled and Phillip . . . well, he fell off the balcony."

"You have got to be kidding me! Was anyone hurt?" I asked.

"No, ma'am, he was too drunk to get hurt." Phillip so needed to go, and so I called Nick, the owner of the apartment complex, to explain what had happened.

"I really can't afford another vacancy right now, so let's just see if Phillip settles down," Nick said.

Well, it wasn't too long after my conversation with Nick when Phillip walked into Logan's apartment in the middle of the night after a drinking binge.

Logan was a chubby and jovial soul in his early thirties with a little premature balding and an accent with sort of a bayou flavor himself, who lived in the small two-bedroom directly below Phillip's apartment.

After a late night of playing his music and being loud and obnoxious out in the parking lot until 3:00 a.m., Phillip had walked into Logan's apartment, drunk and uninvited, waking Logan and his small family. Logan had to physically throw him out, and when Phillip refused to leave the doorway, Logan called the police. When the police arrived, Phillip retaliated, turning the tables on Logan by accusing him of being a drug dealer who had threatened violence. Thank goodness the police didn't believe Phillip and arrest poor Logan right in front of his children. Phillip had after all been Logan's neighbor, and Logan just didn't feel quite right about pressing charges against him, so Phillip was just told to go home and sleep it off. But that wasn't the end of his antics.

Phillip continued to play music and drink in the parking lot at all hours of the night, and on more than one occasion would tell tenants and maintenance people that he was working for the management company.

It was 6:00 a.m. on Sunday and there was Phillip bouncing a broom handle on the floorboards of the apartments above the basement. "What are you doing?" Mrs. Delaney asked Phillip.

"I'm cleanin' the basement for the management company. I work for them now."

And on several occasions, the carpet cleaner or cleaning person would be surprised by Phillip walking into the apartment they were working in.

"Can I help you?" asked Lawrence, the carpet cleaner.

Phillip with his clipboard in hand answered, "No, I'm just the buildin' manager. Just seein' what's needin' to be done to the apartment, and while you're on the property, I need for you to go over to my apartment and clean the carpet."

Lawrence laughed. "No, you're not the building manager, and I don't do anything unless Nancy tells me to."

Phillip left the apartment in a huff, and since Lawrence refused to clean his carpet, later that afternoon, Phillip left me a drunken message on my voice mail.

"Yeah, my faucets leak, there's holes in my walls, and my apartment was never painted. The least you can do is have my carpet cleaned," Phil slurred.

But that's not all.

Phillip blocked elderly Mrs. Delaney's visiting nurse into a parking space because she unknowingly parked in one of his parking spaces. Now Phillip had owned just one vehicle, but it was the principle of it, he said.

Tenants threatened to move because of Phillip's actions and there were rumors that he allowed a runaway girl to live in his apartment, and the list goes on and on.

But the so-called straw that broke the camel's back was the day Phillip began to spread a rumor about *me*!

One afternoon I got an email from Logan telling me that he thought I should know that Phillip was spreading rumors around the tiny apartment complex, about me personally. Yes, the email read that Phillip was going around telling everyone that would listen that their property manager did cocaine. Also, in the same email, Logan said that he was moving his family out of the apartment all the while claiming that it wasn't because of his neighbor, Phillip.

Well, that did it. I had never even tried Cocaine in my life, and now he was attacking me personally. While Nick wouldn't let me kick Phillip out, he sure couldn't stop me from threatening to!

February, 2xxx
Phillip XXXX
000 XXXX
St. Charles, Mo.

Dear Phillip:

This is in regard to several complaints that we have either recently received or have received in the past but were often asked to disregard as the problem had been resolved, but things have escalated to a point that I feel it is necessary to address the situation.

This information did not come from any one person but several sources have reported the following:

The prior tenants below your apartment made complaints of your loud and boisterous behavior but claimed to have worked things out with you yet moved out anyway.

We are told that you play your music late at night, drink in the parking lot, and have been loud as early in the morning as 3:00 a.m. You have been known to give alcohol to minors and a runaway girl lived in your apartment. You awaken neighbors early on weekend mornings, claiming to work for the real estate company.

You have walked into two apartments uninvited after drinking and had to be physically removed in both instances.

You blocked a visiting nurse into your parking space and intimidated both she and your elderly neighbor by shining the headlights of your vehicle into her apartment.

And last but not least, you have tried to destroy my credibility by telling other tenants of my personal habits and business practices of which you know absolutely nothing about and are certainly untrue.

This is to inform you that if this office receives any more complaints or stories about you, you will promptly be given notice to vacate.

> Sincerely,
> N. S. Jordan
> Property Manager

Much to my surprise, I heard nothing out of Phillip for the next few months.

All through the spring and summer, rent was either paid late or paid by different churches and once was even paid by one of Phillip's elderly neighbors for him, which disturbed me. At least there had been no complaints. Maybe he was turning over a new leaf or at least that's what I thought until another dreaded phone message that of course was about none other than you know who.

By now it was the end of August. The night before, Phillip had followed the female guest of another tenant to her car, all the while saying gross and nasty things to her of what he would like to do to her sexually and scaring her to death. The tenant threatened, "If you don't do something about getting this guy out of here, we're gonna move soon as our lease is up!"

I called Nick and told him that if he wanted to keep Phillip as a tenant, then he absolutely would begin losing all his good tenants because, once again, Phillip was up to no good.

"Well, now wait, I understand totally. If you feel like we need to ask Phillip to move, I would much rather have him move than lose other tenants."

That's it? It was as easy as this?

Well, all right then! Not to waste any time I eagerly began to write up Phillip's notice to vacate.

> August, 2xxx
> Notice to vacate
>
> Dear Phillip XXXX
> Please consider this to be your thirty (30)-day notice to vacate the property located at XXXX St. Charles, Mo.

As you know, you had previously been warned that if there were any more incidents that you were involved in, you would be given notice to vacate the abovementioned property.

We have had a recent complaint involving your lewd conduct toward the guest of a neighboring tenant who is now threatening to move out due to your unacceptable behavior.

As your rent is consistently late or being paid by charitable organizations, and with the most recent payment having been paid by one of your elderly neighbors, not to mention that a balance remains unpaid, you are being asked to vacate.

Rather than lose our quiet tenants who pay their rent in a timely manner, we are asking you to vacate the property no later than midnight of September 30.

If you do not comply, legal action will be taken against you and you may be charged double rent for the hold over period as stated in the Missouri Landlord/Tenant Law.

Sincerely,
N. S. Jordan
Property Manager

Well, just a few days past and at 2:00 a.m., Phillip left a message on my voice mail: "We have no lease, so you can't kick me out . . . so, ha!"

Phillip had been on a month-to-month lease so that we could kick him out whenever we so pleased. After hearing Phillip's voice mail, it didn't seem like he was going to leave willingly, and so it was time for none other than legal action.

So I immediately hired an attorney, Mr. Steven A., once again. By now he was certainly becoming all too familiar with the little apartment complex on the edge of town.

A few weeks later Phillip appeared for the first court date, which is the day in which the case is set for trial exactly one week later.

In the meantime, Mr. Steven A. had been doing a little investigating on his own and learned that Phillip had a warrant out for his arrest in New Orleans.

On the day of the trial for rent and possession of Phillip's apartment, Steven met me at the top of the stairs on the third floor of the courthouse building.

"You're not going to believe this," Steven said. "I've been doing some checking on our defendant, and it seems that there is a warrant for his arrest for assault and battery of a former girlfriend in New Orleans. So when Phillip approaches the bench to be sworn in, I've arranged to have him arrested and extradited back to Louisiana."

Wow. I thought, *This has really gotten out of hand. I had never bargained for anything like this to happen and this is really gonna piss Phillip off.*

Throughout the years, there had been times that I had felt uneasy walking to my car in the evening and even while in my own home because of some of the things that tenants had said to me over being kicked out or the nonreturn of a security deposit, like, "You better watch your back," or be awakened by a running car sitting outside of my home.

After Phillip was arrested that day in court, I had many a sleepless night worried whether or not he would come after me, especially after hearing through the grapevine that his giant flat-screen TV had been stolen from his apartment while he was sitting in jail. He never retaliated, but I knew that he was still ever present as odd as it may seem. Once every couple a years or so, someone would call to inquire about rentals and would tell me that Phillip had told them to call me. Creepy, huh?

There were plenty more characters where Phillip came from, there was Mary, who couldn't afford to pay her rent, and so she took every wayward person in from the streets that had a little money and could help her to pay rent. Then there was Waylon, an elderly man diagnosed with schizophrenia who liked to throw the N-word around. He was disturbed by everyone and everything in the little apartment complex. Christine and Christopher, the tenants who lived above him, didn't help matters any. They would agitate their neighbor by stomping on the floorboards upstairs, and their crying children didn't help matters any.

Waylon would become upset and go out into the parking lot and call the first person he saw the N-word no matter what color they were! After the second time he did that, he was promptly asked to leave the neighborhood.

With Waylon no longer there to aggravate, Chris and Christine began to torment the neighbor who lived across the hall from Waylon's old apartment. A young man by the name of Ronnie. Christopher would pound his fist on Ron's wall as he stomped up the staircase or knock on Ron's door and run away. Once Ronnie heard the sound of water splattering outside his door, and there was Christopher peeing in the hallway. Later that evening Ron was in the common area basement doing some laundry when Christopher came and sat on the steps glaring at Ronnie all the while slapping a big flashlight against his leg.

Ronnie, who had become scared of Christopher, ran up the stairs past Christopher and then Chris took chase. Neighbors called the police because there was a man with a flashlight chasing another man through the apartment complex who was screaming and yelling "Call the police!"

Next day Ronnie came into my office, paid the lease break penalty, and informed me that he was out of there! Needless to say, Christopher and Christine were also asked to vacate the premises.

Not long after the vacant apartments were filled and all was well and running smoothly, I received a blessing in disguise. It was a short email from Nick, the owner of the buildings. The email read:

> Dear Nancy,
> I have learned so much from you that I feel like I am able to manage the properties on my

own now, and so please accept this as my notice to terminate your services.

Thanks for everything.

Nick H.

After all the crap I took for him? He terminated our business relationship with an email? Like a schoolboy breaking up with his girlfriend by email or a text message.

Well, so much for favors. But countless times I wanted to give Nick notice that I would no longer manage his properties, and so in the end, the way I looked at it was that by Nick taking his properties back to manage them on his own, he was the one who had done me the favor.

Just as the "Monster Buck" inspired me to write, "The Favor" inspired me to stop writing!

Trapped

Sometimes I stay late at the office. The office is closed, the office is dark, everyone's gone, no phones ringing, no distractions . . .

I'll say it again: the office was dark and everyone's gone and I was just getting ready to lock up and go home when an old Volkswagen Bug whipped in the driveway and sped by. The car sped by and around to the parking lot at the rear of the building, turned around, and parked beside the building.

Three guys got out of the car. Young guys with long hair. Ahh, the '80s, the era of bellbottom blue jeans, guys with long hair, and leisure suits in pastel colors.

Okay, they were probably harmless, but I was only in my middle to late twenties and not bad looking, if I may. I had worn a short skirt with heels, and I wasn't about to walk out into a dark parking lot, knowing three guys were out there.

Peeking out through the heavy curtains of my old manager's office, I could see that the guys were rolling a joint on the engine hood of the car. By now, it's about 7:00 p.m., and all I wanted to do was to go home. They lit up the joint and began to pass it around. Now I could hear laughter and can hear talking, but I couldn't really understand what they're saying. *Tick, tick, tick* . . . Now it's 7:15 p.m., and they're sitting on the curb of the sidewalk along the side of the building. At 7:30 p.m. they've got the munchies and are devouring bags of chips.

"All right now, hard telling how long they're gonna party here and I need to get home to my family," I thought.

Mad at myself for letting this trio of people that I didn't even know ruin my night, I decided to call the cops.

"Emergency," said the voice on the other end of the line.

"Hello, this isn't really an emergency, but I've been waiting to leave my office for forty-five minutes now because there are three guys outside smokin' pot and I'm afraid to go out there."

"We'll send a car your way, ma'am."

So I was looking out the front window of the office, watching for the police to come to my rescue, and I saw the little Volkswagen Bug speed back down the driveway and then I saw the Bug and the police car pass one another on the street. Go figure, but I really didn't want to get the guys in to trouble. I just wanted to go home!

From the police cruiser, a tiny little gal with spikey short blond hair stepped out from behind the car door, so I unlocked the door and met her in the parking lot.

I explained to her that the car that had been in the parking lot for so long had just left. I had even seen the police car and the Volkswagen pass each other on the street.

Not much was said about the three guys smoking pot in the parking lot and our conversation ended with "Do you sell real estate?"

A little puzzled, I said, "Yeah." nodding my head.

"Well, me and my partner are lookin' to buy a house together. Would you be interested in findin' us a house?"

"Of course I would." With that, she handed her card to me and got back in her cruiser, and of course, I skedaddled right out of there before anything else could possibly happen.

After a few months of showing the two gals homes for sale, they finally decided on a small ranch-style home.

If you're a real estate agent, you will think I'm crazy for what I'm about to tell you, but I was actually sorry to see the escrow close. I had a blast those few months showing the two of them around. All we did was joke and laugh.

Too bad all of my escapades in the real estate business couldn't have been as much fun! Oh, but don't get me wrong, being a Realtor® has been and remains to be…a great experience.

The End

About the Author

N. S. Jordan was born in St. Louis in 1957 to a stay-at-home mom, busy raising two kids, and an auto body mechanic, which might explain her passion for automobiles. Nancy has been a full-time million- and multimillion-dollar Missouri Realtor in St. Charles County since 1976 and began the practice of managing rental properties in 1988. During this time, she started to notice some pretty quirky goings on in the world of real estate. One of Nancy's many escapades has been published in a national Realtor publication, and she has been interviewed by a paranormal investigator as well as a newspaper reporter about her ghostly encounters. Nancy has been told by many that she should write a book, and then one day she found herself in such an unusual situation that she was finally compelled to do so.

CPSIA information can be obtained
at www.ICGtesting.com
Printed in the USA
FFHW02n0337300918
48625402-52580FF